Fashion Marketing and Communication

Some of the usual obstacles to modern teachings of marketing are ethnocentricity, the limitation of creative thought by conformity to existing theories, lack of questioning of ethics, and a disconnection from historic events or sociological discourse. This book, in contrast, draws together interdisciplinary approaches from marketing, branding, promotion and critical media studies as tools for understanding the way in which fashion works today, and re-evaluates what makes certain fashion marketing tactics fashionable.

Offering a combination of theory and practice, *Fashion Marketing and Communication* is full of international case studies, practice-based examples and interviews with scholars and practitioners in the fashion and communications industry. Covering subjects including the history of consumerism, fashion marketing, the creative direction of the fashion brand and the use of bloggers and celebrities as marketing tools, this book delineates the opportunities and challenges facing the future of fashion media in the twenty-first century.

Examining the last 100 years of marketing and communications, current theory and practice, as well as questions on the ethics of the fashion industry, this broad-ranging and critical text is perfect for undergraduate and postgraduate students of fashion marketing, branding and communication.

Olga Mitterfellner is an internationally experienced fashion marketing professional and lecturer at London College of Fashion, University of the Arts London, UK. Previously, Olga was Professor of Fashion Management at Mediadesign Hochschule in Munich, Germany. She is a member of the British Sociological Association and a Chartered member of the International Textile Institute.

'The fashion industry is the quintessential example of an industry whose marketing has profoundly shaped and manipulated consumer tastes and, indeed, society. In this intriguing new book, Olga Mitterfellner, a London-based fashion professional and teacher, reviews marketing and communication strategies and methods used in fashion in a refreshing and interesting way. This book includes a multitude of fascinating case studies, connecting fashion marketing to broader marketing principles, through historical and current examples as well as interviews with prominent figures in the fashion world.'

—**Geoffrey Fong**, *Professor of Psychology at the University of Waterloo, Canada*

'This book shows that to be a fashion lover and maintain an activist's heart are not mutually exclusive. The globally-minded concept speaks to an all-too-rare approach to fashion education for the student or professional. It has become commonplace to relate social responsibility to sustainability in the supply chain, but ethics plays a crucial role throughout the entire fashion industry. Olga's chapters blend history and modern practices in marketing to create a better understanding and support progressive change.'

—**Monica Sklar**, *Assistant Professor of Fashion History and Merchandising and Liaison to the Historic Clothing and Textiles Collection at the University of Georgia, USA*

'Mitterfellner carefully takes us through traditional marketing structures, straight through their morph into current techniques of branding, all the while weaving ethical considerations throughout the discipline. Through the lens of an enterprise's social responsibility, her sharp critical eye forces us to consider fashion's journey and cultural impact on the market in which it operates. This book is required reading for any sustainability, fashion management or marketing student. For marketing practitioners, as a moral guide, it must live on one's reference shelf.'

—**Ellen Pabst von Ohain**, *Managing Director of Phoenix Sustainable Communications and Professor of Sustainability and Business, PR and Communications at the European Business School in Munich, Germany*

'Olga Mitterfellner presents a refreshingly honest account of contemporary marketing practices in the global fashion industry that takes account of their historical origins and global application. Her account of this alluring but sometimes brutal sector presents a balanced perspective of the paradoxical relationship between commercial and ethical imperatives at play in fashion. This comprehensive, easy-to-read text is distinctive in the modern fashion setting and is a must-read for industry practitioners, students of fashion marketing and those keen to understand how we got to where we are now.'

—*Tony Cooper, Lecturer in Fashion Marketing at the London College of Fashion, University of the Arts London, UK*

'Professor Mitterfellner takes the subject of fashion marketing and communications and illustrates the whole process from early examples of historical PR to the impact of social media on modern consumerism, traditional marketing techniques to the cynicism of targeted advertising through selling aspirational lifestyles, and finally what the future holds for this most embedded form of outreach from the retailers. This book is an ideal text for students and practitioners alike.'

—*Rebecca Unsworth, Executive Director for The Textile Institute, UK*

'This impressive book has a refreshing look at the fundamentals of theory and practice coupled with the past and present developments of Fashion Marketing. Students and practitioners will learn, explore, and re-evaluate the industry as Olga Mitterfellner has expertly added a much needed dialog on ethics in marketing, prompting us to think and work responsibly.'

—*Ilan Alon, Professor of Strategy and International Marketing and Head of International Affairs at the University of Agder, Norway*

Fashion Marketing and Communication

Theory and Practice Across the Fashion Industry

OLGA MITTERFELLNER

LONDON AND NEW YORK

First published 2020
by Routledge
2 Park Square, Milton Park, Abingdon, Oxon OX14 4RN

and by Routledge
52 Vanderbilt Avenue, New York, NY 10017

Routledge is an imprint of the Taylor & Francis Group, an informa business

British Library Cataloguing-in-Publication Data
A catalogue record for this book is available from the British Library

Library of Congress Cataloging-in-Publication Data
Names: Mitterfellner, Olga, 1978– author.
Title: Fashion marketing and communication : theory and practice across the
fashion industry / Olga Mitterfellner.
Description: Abingdon, Oxon ; New York, NY : Routledge, 2020. |
Includes bibliographical references and index.
Identifiers: LCCN 2019028144 (print) | LCCN 2019028145 (ebook) |
ISBN 9781138323087 (hardback) | ISBN 9781138323094 (paperback) |
ISBN 9780429451591 (ebook) Subjects: LCSH: Fashion merchandising. |
Advertising–Fashion. | Clothing trade. | Communication in marketing. |
Branding (Marketing) Classification: LCC HF6161.C44 M59 2020 (print) |
LCC HF6161.C44 (ebook) | DDC 746.9/20688–dc23
LC record available at https://lccn.loc.gov/2019028144
LC ebook record available at https://lccn.loc.gov/2019028145

ISBN: 978-1-138-32308-7 (hbk)
ISBN: 978-1-138-32309-4 (pbk)
ISBN: 978-0-429-45159-1 (ebk)

Typeset in Dante and Avenir
by Newgen Publishing UK

Visit the eResources: www.routledge.com/9781138323094

Dedication

This book is dedicated to all my past, present and future students who teach me so much. They inspire me to keep believing in their bright future within the fashion industry. It was not without their curiosity, intelligence, dedication and motivation that I found enough patience to write so many pages (or understand why FOMO is a major concern).

Education is what can lift anyone above and beyond their limits and I hope that the contents will do just that: elevate each reader both intellectually and personally. On that note I must also thank my family, mentors and friends for cheering me on in all my endeavours and never tiring of an intellectual conversation.

Furthermore, I dedicate this book to all those (humans and animals) who have been wronged by the fashion industry and its unethical practices. I cannot fully feel your pain, but I can try and improve on the past and hopefully change the future.

Finally, I dedicate this book to my late step-father Georgi Nikolayevich Vladimov, who was awarded the Russian Booker Prize and the Sakharov Prize: everything you said is true.

Contents

About this book

Anyone who is interested in both fashion marketing and communications will find a comprehensive introduction to relevant fields of interest and understand how brands use marketing and communication strategies in the industry. Whether a practitioner or a student, you can find fresh, different ideas and sometimes a radical and unusual perspective on the subject matter.

However, this is not just a standard book which explains fashion marketing, branding and communication, but also an invitation to build your own expert opinion by exploring the past, questioning the present and contemplating the future of the industry.

This book takes a unique angle on fashion marketing, in contrast to many books which are focused on current practices and trends – surely important – because only a very few take the reader back to its origins. These origins are of significance because they are the foundation of modern marketing and only by understanding these origins and evolement can a person evaluate modern practices and make an informed ethical judgement. By exploring these historical elements, one can become a cultured person – first and foremost – and then a professional marketer, capable of conducting an educated discourse on a variety of topics. The theory is coupled with short case examples from around the world, contextualizing some unusual approaches in practice.

Each chapter also invites the reader to reflect on ethical considerations. The Merriam-Webster definition (2019) of ethics is "the discipline dealing with what is good and bad and with moral duty and obligation" and it is that very moral obligation that marketing tutors, students and practitioners have.

This is because every aspiring marketing professional and current marketer needs to be aware of the complex ethical implications of the profession. Many products and services which are marketed, and in fashion specifically, can have unethical traits and even cause harm. Sometimes the negative effects are not immediately evident in daily professional life. With this book, you can consider the pros and cons and make up your own opinion of marketing practices. You can alter your course, change behaviour and implement a best-practice approach in your career. Hopefully, this book will encourage each reader to be the most ethically responsible marketer and make a difference in the world.

Furthermore, each chapter is specifically designed to explore content independently from each other, allowing readers to pick and choose areas of interest without having to power through it from beginning to end.

Finally, the book has interviews with subject specialists and industry experts – real people who work in the real industry – from the UK, Germany, the USA and Russia, offering their unique insights and a more global outlook on various topics.

Preface

How to teach fashion when you stop believing in fashion? This is what I asked myself when I was awarded a professorship in Fashion Management in 2015.

Fashion. It is a world of glitz and glam, fairy tales and extravaganza. Modern fashion of the last few decades needs the combination of creativity, smart business strategies and lots of brand hype in order to exist. I used to be someone who just loved loved loved loved! the new it-bag or absolutely had to have those high heels fresh off the catwalk, which only the coolest fashionistas of the world's capitals knew about. Attending amaaaazing fashion shows, running my own small label and doing my very own shows, mixing with the "right crowd" and following the most important trends used to be my thing when I was younger.

At some point, however, and after many years of working in the industry, I learned that this is a deceptive industry, a huge multi-billion-pound business, selling us a world of luxury, make-believe, unattainable beauty and dream aspirations. It's not all gold that glitters, you can say, and it can be equally unfair on the consumers as well as on the creators, let alone the environment.

Let's start with the designers. The most talented creative minds can easily still live in a flat share well into their 30s and freelance from one job to the other, hoping to make it big one day or at least pay the next bill in the meantime. (They might have masterminded that iconic T-shirt print last season, but they won't get credit for it.) Sometimes it's your connections that help you land that job and not your honestly-earned degree. Sometimes despite the connections it all fails. Quite a few big designers have declared bankruptcy during their way up, including Yves-Saint-Laurent, Christian Lacroix and Valentino just to name a few.

How about the imagery, advertising and PR? In my many years of working in the industry, I've learned that the most celebrated fashion models can end up used and forgotten within a few seasons (or even dead due to size 0) and it turns out that magazines and Photoshop are best friends who want consumers to believe in unattainable beauty standards, destroying their own physical and psychological health. Marketing is manipulative and uncanny unless someone or something regulates it.

And while we flood the high streets in order to buy whatever the magazines write about, we rarely think about the ones who sewed the clothes. The extreme mark-up is hardly ever justified when you look at true production cost.

There is a lot of truth to TV series like Ugly Betty or the famous movie about an iconic editor-in-chief who wears Prada. I remember a friend who was not in the fashion industry asking me: "Are people really like that in the fashion industry?" I smiled and replied: "Of course not! They are much much worse!" Such were my observations and experiences, that at some point I felt like I did not believe in fashion anymore.

When I was asked to teach about fashion in a university, I had to figure out why, what and how to teach fashion. After all, these young students who signed up for my classes would consider a career in the industry and need motivation on their way.

So in order to get my mind back into the wonderful world of fashion, I slowly started looking at those elements which I still loved about fashion. I went through my own vast library of movies, books and magazines on fashion, of which some I had not touched in years. Books on design, books on marketing, books on advertising, on trends. My own wardrobe, my textile and fashion creations as well as files of work and research compiled for clients, drawings, brand books and media reports were my treasure vault of all things amazing.

Then there were my own files from my time as an MA student at Central Saint Martins in London. Our year group was so eager and did amazing work. It was during those MA years that I began to question the ethical practices of the fashion industry, the manipulative nature of marketing and the harmful imagery of advertising and PR. This critical approach did not disappear but grew stronger over the professional years and this was what gave me the why, what and how to teach about fashion.

Why? To convey something that my own education did: An ethical, critical and inquisitive approach, looking into history and taking this into the future!

What? The industry in all its many facettes, how it works, how people work in it, how theory applies and what reality looks like. All of the good and the bad.

How? With a mix of inspiring facts, intriguing questions, fascinating history, budding trends, with the help of guest experts, with our own classroom questions and creative answers.

Now, having taught fashion for many years, I am putting the Why – What – How into a book to share with brilliant minds around the world and appreciate each reader for taking the time to critically think about the topics presented. Fashion and the industry can be enjoyed by practitioners and consumers alike. It has a great influence on us, so let's treat it with great responsibility.

Last but not least, please note that on occasion you may find small errors in the text and I ask you in advance for consideration and forgiveness, since English is my third language out of five.

Fashion marketing from a historical perspective

1

Early days of advertising and consumerism

Chapter topics

How to define fashion marketing?

Marketing, and specifically fashion marketing, is part of a large industry – the fashion system – and it has a long-standing history dating back hundreds of years as well as practices which are just a few decades old. The fashion system can be seen as a 'Fashion Carousel' because it is a cyclical system which is ever changing whilst it recycles ideas from the past. It consists of elements such as textiles, design, production, retail, marketing, media, culture and history, but also trends and future forecasts. (The Carousel here will be revisited in the last chapter of the book.)

Fashion marketing in particular can take many forms and many expressions, so in order to understand the place where marketing sits within the fashion system, it is necessary to look at a few definitions that try to accurately describe it.

One such definition states:

> The fashion system offers a "structure, organisation and processes employed to conceive, create, produce, distribute, communicate, retail and consume fashion. [It] embodies the full supply chain of fashion and includes not only the individual components, (what the action is) but also the methods adopted to enable and realise each activity (how it is being done)".
>
> (Vecchi and Buckley, 2016)

This is a modern definition which describes the design and production of fashion, sourcing of materials, distribution and retailing (both offline and online) and consumption of fashion with all its methodology, such as marketing, advertising and PR. The marketing of fashion specifically takes care of taking the product and getting it to the consumers, at the right price, in the right place and by successfully promoting. These consumers – existing and potential ones – are essentially "the market".

It ties in with the "Marketing Mix", which is explored in Chapter 3 in more detail. Originally it was McCarthy who separated Marketing Mix activities into four broad categories or elements, which he called the 4Ps of marketing: product, price, place and promotion. Later, the four Marketing Mix elements were expanded to 7Ps, which included process, physical evidence and people (Kotler *et al.* 2009, p.17).

An alternative definition adds a cultural and sociological aspect to the fashion system: "The fashion industry forms part of a larger social and cultural phenomenon known as the 'fashion system,' a concept that embraces not only the business of fashion but also the art and craft of fashion, and not only production but also consumption" (*Encyclopedia Britannica*, 2018).

The rather complex sociological aspects of fashion theory have been written about by authors such as Roland Barthes, Bourdieu, Lipovetsy, Simmel, Veblen, Baudrillard, just to name a few. A perhaps more accessible author for fashion students is Yuniya Kawamura who wrote about the phenomenon of "Fashion-ology" in a modern context. Fashion-ology, according to Kawamura, is a study of fashion but it does not focus on the apparel or process as such. Her intent is the sociological investigation of fashion (Kawamura, 2005).

In order to understand the historical setting that brought us fashion marketing and the relevant communications practice, in this book we look at marketing as it initially emerged, moving on to modern practice. There is a focus on the way marketing is used to communicate with consumers, methods used and their implications.

The history of advertising, particularly in the nineteenth and twentieth centuries

The marketing methods in order to reach the consumers, such as the promotion of products through advertising and public relations, can arguably be traced back many centuries, if not millennia into human history.

Ever since people went to market they engaged in marketing their goods and communicating with potential and actual consumers.

About 2000–1000 BC, written advertising was recorded in places such as ancient Rome and Greece on clay boards or on artefacts. In many cultures around the world, there was a primal form of advertising (especially where literacy was absent) and this might have meant shouting loudly at the market to get shoppers' attention for one's produce. This would of course only reach people in the immediate vicinity of the market and was far from the global marketing we know today with large billboards, branded goods, jingles and digital channels.

Europe's development in particular was held up by the Dark Ages, where for the duration of nearly 1000 years, all but the clergy and aristocracy had forgotten literacy once acquired from ancient Greece and Rome. Any significant development pertaining to marketing was practically frozen during this millennium.

Then came the re-birth of Europe: The Renaissance. Early modern Europe began with the invention of the printing press by Gutenberg in the fifteenth century and gave way for mass-printed text which could be circulated to a broader audience. There is some evidence of so-called "Flyposting" in Europe in the fifteenth century which is somewhat similar to posters or billboards with text on it. However, in Europe the people who could actually read were still very scarce and so only in the nineteenth century was literacy integrated into the educational system and spread wide enough for most people to be able to read printed text and the subsequent ads (Kloss, 2012). This means that despite the mechanical invention of creating print, advertising in written form could only begin much later as the communicator of the message and recipient first had to be on a similar level of literacy. (The communications theory will be discussed further in Chapter 6.)

Table 1.1 History of advertising

Medium	Dating back to*	Still in use today?
Magazines (Print)	18th century	Yes
Newspapers (Print)	18th century	Yes
Billboards and Posters	From 1850s (Flyposting from 15th century in Europe)	Yes
Radio	From 1920	Yes
Silent Film (Cinema)	End of 19th century	No
Sound Film (Cinema)	From 1920s	Yes
Illuminated Advertising (later neon signs)	End of 19th century	Yes
Radio	From 1920s	Yes
Television	From 1920s	Yes
Internet and Digital	From 1990s onwards	Yes

Up to the nineteenth century however, one might argue that advertising was not a necessity anyway as consumption of goods was restricted to the essentials which means that people only bought what they needed and in small quantities. In this respect, local and limited scope advertising sufficed because consumers were personally acquainted with the butcher, the baker or the grocer, and the hat maker chose their place of purchase based on what was available in proximity, how good the product was, and how much they liked and trusted the producer of the goods.

As for fashion, people either made garments themselves if they knew how to weave or knit, or they purchased expensive cloth from someone who did and then made a garment which would hopefully last them most of their life so that they could pass it on to the next person. The sartorial consumption was of course different for aristocracy and upper class citizens who had more choice and more garments than most of the other citizens.

How the industrial revolution led to present marketing practices

Then, at the end of the eighteenth century until the middle of the nineteenth century, the industrial revolution happened: When the UK and US started to make great inventions such as the steam engine or textile weaving machines and found the right type of fuel to power the machines (steam, coal, electricity etc.) the production of many goods became mechanized.

Replacing human labour with machines meant that the output could be increased tremendously. Thus, factories emerged, putting children, women and men into the workplace.

It must be remembered that the working conditions were poor and dangerous, the hours were long and there were no unions to look after the workers' rights. It was normal to work for 14 hours on six days a week, no matter if you were a child or an adult, using dangerous machines and chemicals. In fact, this might sound familiar to you if you have been following the labour conditions of modern fashion production facilities in developing countries. What we perceive as an atrocity now, is an invention from around 200 years ago, tried and tested by the first entrepreneurs and part of an era known as early democratic capitalism. The appalling working conditions of the industrial revolution went on for over a century and sometimes more, before people were able to force the proprietors to make the workplace safer and conditions better by joining up in unions, walking out to demonstrate or going on strike.

Henry Ford was one of the first people to have introduced assembly lines which could move (an early equivalent of today's conveyor-belt) at Ford Motor Company's Highland Park, Michigan factory in 1908 (Lemelson-MIT, n.d.).

With the subsequent use of the conveyor belt in many factories, the huge and fast output of goods increased dramatically. The masses of consumer goods were then transported to many stores, often far away so that the producer and consumer no longer knew each other and products were being sold to an "unknown" customer (Zeit Online, 1955).

Figure 1.1 Textile mill. Image Credit: Pixabay.

The huge output beyond basic needs meant that there was an imbalance of supply and demand.

Ideally, the supply of manufactured goods and the demand for goods should be in balance. In some cases, supply was scarce so that people had to queue for basic goods such as food, which often happened during economic times of hardship and war.

In the case of the industrial revolution, suddenly more goods were being rapidly produced whilst people had no real need to increase consumption. Supply and demand fell out of balance (the imbalance is shown in Figure 1.3). Now there was no harmony between seller and buyer, no buyers had to queue for goods, but on the contrary, the manufacturers had to make an effort to gain the customers' attention and secure a sale.

Thus manufacturers of goods had two new tasks: One was to encourage people to become consumers of more goods than they actually need and increase

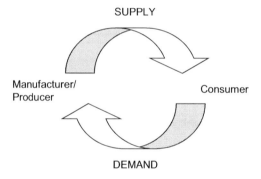

Figure 1.2 The balance of supply and demand pre-industrial revolution.

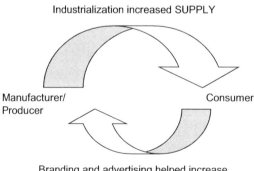

Figure 1.3 The balance of supply and demand post-industrial revolution.

demand. The other was to distinguish their product from the competitors so that their products would be preferred over others.

The origin of modern-day consumerism and brands

As a result of the industrialization, from the middle of the nineteenth century onwards, and in particular in the years around the turn of the twentieth century, the strategic profession of branding and advertising began to emerge as two instruments which would enable consumerism. In fact, advertising was thriving and between 1867 and 1890, in the USA it grew tenfold whilst similar growth was happening in industrial and advanced countries such as the UK (Kloss, 2012 p.35). In order to distinguish themselves from competitors, manufacturers began to brand their goods. According to the American Marketing Association "A brand is a name, term, design, symbol, or any other feature that identifies one seller's good or service as distinct from those of other sellers".

As brands became increasingly competitive amongst each other they soon began employing specialists who would design the best possible strategies in order to outwit the competitors and engage the consumer and the USA had a huge pioneering role in advertising and branding, which is why many textbooks on marketing will have a US-bias. In fact, marketing professor and author of many marketing textbooks Philip Kotler (2012) finds the roots of marketing to be quite an American commodity.

But how exactly could advertising get the brand's message through to its existing and potential customer? Which channels could a brand use if it was no longer based in its local shop or in a market stall, shouting out loudly? Here another vital necessity for modern-day advertising came into play: mass media. Newspapers, and railroads for distributing newspapers created the necessary infrastructure for modern mass communication in the twentieth century.

The development of different media channels for advertising began with print media such as the poster, the billboard, newspapers and magazines. *Vogue* magazine was a newspaper at first when it appeared in 1892; the *Ladies' Home Journal* had been founded in 1883 (Breward, 1994).

However, in France and England, fashion magazines had been around since the turn of the eighteenth century such as the French journal *Le journal des dames et des modes*.

Advertising for products in the first mail order catalogues emerged around the same time, such as the Sears catalogue.

The industrial revolution equally influenced infrastructure and transportation, which means that there were suddenly new effective methods to spread printed media very quickly across entire countries, including large territories such as the USA. The construction of railroads, which could distribute printed media quickly all over the country, or even across borders, if necessary, was a facilitator for advertising to really take off and grow. Steam heat and electric lights started to replace stoves as well as oil and gas lamps in the 1880s whilst just 10 years later electric locomotives appeared.

The *Historical Guide to North-American Railroads* (1985) describes this sudden industrial advancement of transport and infrastructure that took place roughly at the end of the nineteenth century.

Interestingly, before the turn of the nineteenth century, American cities and railroads used a large number of different time zones. Each train station thus set its own clock, making it difficult to coordinate train schedules and once travel was reduced from an entire day's travel to a few hours, passengers would be easily confused about the time zones.

> A few minutes difference in time between neighbouring cities made little difference when the cities were a day's travel apart. Railroads reduced the time between cities to hours, and the telegraph that accompanied them provided instant communication. To eliminate the confusion […] in 1883 the railroads divided the U.S. into four zones with uniform times an hour apart. Gradually others adopted the standard time of the railroads.
>
> (Drury, 1985, p.8)

The reduced time of transportation did not only influence travel, but also the speed of media distribution to the readers, making communication more rapid. Lane notes that in the USA, by the 1880s over 11,000 different newspapers were available and by 1900 a well-read newspaper such as the *Chicago Tribune* could reach about 50,000 readers. All newspapers contained advertising of course (Lane, 2008).

Radio advertising began to emerge from the early 1920s onwards and with radios being bought by many households they could be used to reach the masses from the pin-point of a single radio station. Radios were also effective in targeting specific customer groups by means of special-interest radio stations.

Case example: Yiddish Radio advertising

An interesting example of targeted fashion advertising on the radio is Yiddish Radio:

> In the beginning of the twentieth century, Jewish immigrants came to America from Eastern Europe in numbers of more than two million people. As the *Yiddish Radio Project* recalls, Yiddish was the

language which connected those immigrants. "The recent Jewish immigrants embraced the medium, and by the early 1930s, Yiddish radio flourished nationwide. In New York alone, 23 stations broadcast dramas, variety programs, man-on-the street interviews, music, commercials, even editorials in rhyme".

(Yiddish Radio Project, 2002)

The radio programs were not only filled with music and entertainment but of course, advertising. Radio time was sold to companies that wanted air-time.

This radio advertising included early forms of fashion advertising – for shops and products all located in the US capital of fashion, New York, and in the immediate neighbourhood of the listeners. Listening to the recordings of those commercials now, you feel the scope of fashion and its significance in the retail landscape of New York's 1930s. From shoes to clothing stores, to famous personalities singing the skits such as cantor Moishe Oisher who sang the theme song of the Stanton Street Clothier (Yiddish Radio Project, 2002). Male and female shoppers were both addressed.

There was a melodic jingle about Old Man's Adler's Elevator shoes on the Jewish Radio Hour which catered to a short man. Elevator shoes can "elevate" the wearer by a few centimetres as they have insoles which are thickened and form a wedge (known as shoe lifts) under the heels. This shoe also promised discreetness to short men who, unlike women, could not simply elevate their height by openly wearing high heels.

In 1947, *Life Magazine* published a story on the Adler elevator shoes radio commercial and the man who was famous for delivering them: Henry Morgan. Morgan's skits were funny and even silly, which made Mr Adler initially quite sceptical about the ads. However, soon after the radio ads began, people flocked to his shop, stating that Morgan had sent them and was asking for Old Man Adler. Subsequently Adler's profits increased (*Life Magazine*, 14 Apr 1947, p.60).

From the turn of the twentieth century, poster, print and radio advertising was joined by moving pictures in silent films and later by the "talking pictures" in the 1920s:

In 1895, the Lumière Cinématographe (Camera) was shown to la Société d'encouragement pour l'industrie nationale, rue de Rennes, in Paris, together with the very first silent film: "La Sortie des usines Lumière" (The exit of the Lumiére factory) by the Lumiere brothers (Lewino and

Table 1.2   American thinkers and pioneers of modern marketing

Name	Lifespan	Contribution to modern marketing
Ivy Lee	1877–1934	First PR activities in the USA
Edward Bernays	1891–1995	Principles of psychology used for PR
Walter Dill Scott	1869–1955	Principles of psychology used for advertising
Ernest Dichter	1907–1991	Principles of psychology used for marketing
Elias St. Elmo Lewis	1872–1948	Inventor of the AIDA-Model
Neil Borden	1895–1980	Inventor of the "Marketing Mix"
E. Jerome McCarthy	1928–2015	Inventor of the 4Ps
Abraham Maslow	1908–1970	Founder of humanistic psychology and Maslow's hierarchy of needs

Dos Santos, 2015). In the same year they publicly showed films, charging a fee from the viewers – the idea of the cinema was born. Feature Films followed about 10 years later with the introduction of cinema ads in the 1920s.

Radio and cinema advertising was predominant for several consecutive decades, rather than TV. Although televisions were already available from the 1920s, they only became a household staple from the 1950s onwards, in countries such as the USA, offering TV advertisements directly in the home. Compared to all other media channels, once accessible by the masses this one grew the fastest and attracted high spending by advertisers (Kloss, 2012; Lane 2013).

And until the 1990s, when internet was introduced as a new technological platform for advertising, these original advertising media channels remained virtually unchanged, still being widely used to this day:

Case example: DeBeers

"A diamond is forever", said a famous advertising agency to America in the 1940s. And everybody believed it without ever asking why.

Women suddenly expected diamond jewellery as an engagement present. Men felt that this is the only way they could propose to their loved one. Hollywood stars suddenly began to wear diamonds and entire movie scripts were built around the precious stone, which we regularly see on the red carpet even today. All thanks to the New York-based ad agency N.W. Ayer and its client De Beers, whose profits rose to $2.1bn by 1979 thanks

Figure 1.4 A Diamond is Forever, 1955. Ad created by N.W. Ayer for De Beers. Image kindly provided by De Beers; photography by Irving Penn.

to one exceptional advertising and marketing campaign that was launched in the 1940s (*The Atlantic*, 2015).

The image shown here is one of many beautiful photographs shot by the now deceased and famed fashion photographer Irving Penn as a series of ads for De Beers. In this image, we are peeking in from behind a palm tree plant, on an intimate moment in the relationship between a woman and a man in a glamorous public place, which – incidentally – is reinforced through a diamond gift. The copy text reads: "When love is new, and lovers share their dreams of life to be, each moment brims with happiness. It's a time that they'll recall, always, in the joyous flames of her engagement diamond". Below four sizes of sparkling diamonds the man can choose from it boldly states: A DIAMOND IS FOREVER.

You might possibly call this an early *integrated marketing* campaign because it not only featured the classic advertising and the copy text, but also used celebrity endorsement by stars, product placement in the cinema and brand ambassadors such as first ladies and the Queen Elizabeth. Whichever store you chose to buy your diamond jewellery from, the stones were by De Beers (Epstein, 1982). This helped to catapult a glitzy stone to stardom and make it synonymous with love, engagement, marriage and the eternal word "forever".

Yet still, hardly anyone asked why one should keep diamonds forever. Critics such as Edward Jay Epstein have said that the true reason was not a celebration of eternal love, but a marketing ploy:

> At the end of the 19th Century there was an ample supply of diamonds in the world and the price for the stone had been raised artificially, which would tumble immediately if everyone tried to resell their diamonds. Furthermore, De Beers controlled the supply and demand of a monopoly. "De Beers had to endow these stones with a sentiment that would inhibit the public from ever reselling them. The illusion had to be created that diamonds were forever – "forever" in the sense that they should never be resold".
>
> (Epstein, 2015)

The USA was one of the pioneers when it came to post-industrial advertising and many ideas, practices and case studies – which are still applicable to this day – stem from there. The first advertising agencies emerged in the latter half of the nineteenth century, such as J. Walter Thompson (founded in 1864 and still active today) and N.W. Ayer & Sons.

At the end of the nineteenth century and in the first decades of the twentieth century, when there was already an industry with many advertising and marketing professionals in the USA, professionals teamed up and founded numerous associations as well as something we'd now call "think tanks". Remarkably, most of them exist until today and have grown considerably, attracting more industry members in equal proportion to the immense growth that the advertising industry experienced in the twentieth century. The members come from all areas and industries, including the fashion industry.

1) The Advertising Club of New York, founded in 1915

    In 1896, a small number of advertising men in New York City began meeting on a regular basis to share ideas on their advertising practices. In 1906 the growing group incorporated as the Advertising Men's League, ultimately becoming The Advertising Club of New York in 1915 thus celebrating 120 years of existence in 2016. Since the 1960s, the club has been giving out the ANDY award to: "[…] honour global creativity in advertising, and recognize the contributions of individuals and companies who continually innovate, experiment and inspire with novel approaches to communication […]" (Advertising Club, 2015).

    The corporate members in 2016 include most of the large advertising agencies of the world such as BBDO, DDD Worldwide, J. Walter Thompson, McCann, Ogilvy & Mather, Publicis, TBWA and Young & Rubicam. TBWA for example, creates advertising for clients such as Adidas and Apple, and J. Walter Thompson – one of the oldest and largest ad agencies in the world – created a docu-fiction for the famous Italian fashion school Istituto Marangoni and featured Italian *Vogue* editor Franca Sozzani.

2) The American Advertising Federation (AAF) founded in 1905

    This organization is based in Washington, DC and claims today that it is "the unifying voice for advertising", because it provides opportunities for professionals from across the vast scope of the profession to build supportive relationships with others in the advertising industry. To accomplish their mission they engage in grassroots activities in order to promote and protect its advertising activities at all levels of government. It counts around 40000 members in 2016 (AAF, "Who we are", 2016).

    It's corporate members include publishers Condé Nast, owners of fashion magazines *GQ*, *Self*, *Teen Vogue*, *Vanity Fair*, *Vogue*, *W* and *Wired* and Hearst Magazines, owners of fashion magazines *Marie Claire*, *Elle*, *Cosmopolitan*, *Esquire*, *Seventeen* and *Harpers Bazaar*.

3) The Association of National Advertisers (ANA), founded in 1910

    It is one of the US advertising industry's oldest trade associations. Today the ANA's membership includes nearly 1000 companies with 15,000 brands that collectively spend or support more than $300 billion in marketing and advertising annually.

    Some of the current members are fashion and beauty companies, including JCPenney, L'Oréal USA, Mary Kay Inc., L Brands (owners of Victoria's Secret, Lasenza and Henri Bendel) and Walmart Stores (ANA, 2016).

4) The American Association of Advertising Agencies (AAAA, 4As), founded in 1917

It was founded in New York as a national trade association to represent US advertising agencies and claims on its website that today "4A's members are responsible for about 80 percent of the total advertising placed by agencies nationwide" (4As, 2016).

Some of AAAA's clients closely work with fashion brands: Luxe Collective Group, a media agency, has done work for Hermes, Karl by Karl Lagerfeld, John Hardy as well as luxury watchmakers such as Blancpain and Breguet. Branding experts Select World have a project portfolio which includes luxury fashion brands Balenciaga, Roberto Cavalli, Marni, Ermenegildo Zegna and Joop!

5) The Advertising Research Foundation (ARF) founded in 1936

Founded in 1936 by the Association of National Advertisers and the American Association of Advertising Agencies, this is a non-profit industry association for sharing knowledge in the fields of advertising and media. Its stated mission is the active development of "leading and bleeding-edge solutions" and to "evangelize the leaders that lead them into action". The ARF wants to "challenge conventions and discover new insights that benefit our member network". Its membership today consists of over 400 advertisers, advertising agencies, research firms, media companies, educational institutions and international organizations and there are a few fashion brands amongst those: Levi Strauss & Co., Nike and retailer Walmart.

It also publishes the academic *Journal of Advertising Research* and has renowned academic members such as Stanford University, New York University and New York Institute of Technology as well as the Wharton School.

(The ARF, 2016)

Equally, similar associations were formed in Europe, such as the Advertising Association in the UK which was founded in 1924, the Reichsverband der Anzeigenvertreter e.V. founded in the 1920s in Germany. In France L'Autorité de Régulation Professionnelle de la Publicité (ARPP) was founded in 1935. However, it was in the USA that the advertising industry was thriving exceptionally well in this particular time period. It also benefitted from early studies in psychology and disciples of Sigmund Freud (who either had studied directly with him or learned his theories) arriving in America and applying psychology to consumer behaviour. Famous thinkers of the early twentieth century (mostly active from the turn of the twentieth century onwards) were Walter Dill Scott, Edward Bernays, Ernest Dichter, Neil Borden and E. Jerome McCarthy, Ivy Lee, Elmo Lewis and Abraham Maslow.

Their contributions to modern marketing practices were highly progressive and significant as most of their theories are used to this day and in the case of the AIDA Model, have been used for more than 110 years. Of course, their ideas have undergone modification and further development, but just like the theories of Sigmund Freud, as a foundation they are still relevant.

Despite the benefits that their work provided for marketing as a new discipline, there are also many reasons why these marketing men were highly criticized. Their practices were often unethical and harmful to the masses, as they were based on manipulation, propaganda and disrespect for the individual physical and psychological health that is in stark contrast to the original ideas of Freud. The influences and consequences of some of these practices are discussed in the next chapters.

Ethical considerations

The rate of fashion production and consumption has seen a stark transformation since the industrial revolution, increasing both to a point where we now have the phenomenon of accelerated production, consumption and the discarding of clothing, entitled "fast fashion" and "throwaway fashion". Equally, today, many fashion brands and activists talk about sustainability and how to improve the fashion industry so that there is less pollution and waste from our accelerated consumption habits.

Arguably, some experts believe that the true problems of today's fashion industry lie in our long-standing habit of consuming – since the industrial revolution – causing global problems such as pollution, production controversies and waste on land and in oceans. In most developed countries we are now used to fashion consumption as a learned behaviour, difficult if not impossible to unlearn.

In fact, in 2017 Greenpeace stated that in order to break our fast-fashion addiction, we have to embrace "true materialism". The group is referring to a book by author Kate Fletcher *Craft of Use*, which describes true materialism as "a switch from an idea of a consumer society where materials matter little, to a truly material society, where materials—and the world they rely on—are cherished". This means treasuring the materials we possess, not discarding them and curbing new purchases.

And if it was not for the industrial revolution and invention of mass media instruments such as newspapers (and transportation for their distribution), cinema, TV and radio, advertising would not have such power and influence over masses of people simultaneously.

> In terms of advertising emerging as a tool to reach consumers, it is imperative to acknowledge its power: As illustrated through the example of the "Diamonds are forever" campaign, it becomes evident that advertising can change society and manipulate our behaviour, even influencing the romantic behaviour of people.

Further reading

Bernays, E. and Miller, M. C. (2004) *Propaganda*. New York: Ig Publishing.

Diamond, J. (2015) *Retail Advertising and Promotion*. New York: Fairchild.

Dichter, E. (1971) *Motivating Human Behavior*. New York: McGraw-Hill.

Heimann, J. and Nieder, A. A. (2016) *20th-Century Fashion: 100 Years of Apparel Ads*. Cologne, Germany: Taschen.

History of Advertising Trust (Learning Resources) www.hatads.org.uk

Lane, W. R., Whitehill Kink, K. and Russel, T. J. (2008) *Kleppner's Advertising Procedure*. 17th edn. New Jersey: Pearson Prentice Hall.

Laird, P. (2001) *Advertising Progress*. Baltimore: Johns Hopkins University Press.

The Atlantic (2015) How an Ad Campaign Invented the Diamond Engagement Ring. www.theatlantic.com/international/archive/2015/02/how-an-ad-campaign-invented-the-diamond-engagement-ring/385376

Tungate, M. (2007) *Adland: A Global History of Advertising*. London: Kogan Page.

Tye, L. (2002) *The Father of Spin: Edward L. Bernays and the Birth of Public Relations*. New York: Henry Holt.

Veblen, T. (2005) *Conspicuous Consumption*. London: Penguin.

Yiddish Radio Project (2002) Sound Portraits Productions. www.yiddishradioproject.org

Fashion promotion and public relations   **2**

Chapter topics

The early days of public relations

Public relations has been present in our history for some centuries but before the 1940s and in the early days it was called propaganda. This is because of the original Latin definition of propaganda or propagare which translates to propagate in English. What does it mean, to propagate? According to the Macmillan Dictionary (2019) it means "to spread ideas, beliefs etc to a lot of people".

Propaganda:

> Macmillian (2019) defines the modern definition of propaganda as "information, especially false information, that a government or organization spreads in order to influence people's opinions and beliefs".

Public relations:

> However, the modern definition of public relations is: "Communication with various internal and external publics to create an image for a product or corporation" (Lane, 2008).

In both the original form of propaganda and in modern public relations there is an organization of political or commercial interest which wants to spread information in order to shape the opinion of the public. Tracing the use of propaganda back a few centuries, Cull, Culbert and Welsh find evidence in the 1500s during in their attempt to create a "Historical Encyclopedia" of such events. One example from those early days is Queen Elizabeth I who employed propagandists and cleverly shaped her relationship with the general public. This is particularly interesting because her "PR strategy" had a strong emphasis on fashion and thus connects the past to the present.

Case example: Queen Elizabeth I

So how exactly does propaganda and PR work in the sixteenth century when Queen Elizabeth I reigned?

There was great pressure on Queen Elizabeth to marry as the political stability of the country and international relations depended on it. However, in the middle of the sixteenth century, it became evident that she was not going to marry and remain a single woman and ruler, which caused much mistrust and discontent.

She is said to have used clever rhetoric (which you could also call propaganda) to persuade parliament to respect her decision. But that was not enough because she had to make her choice viable to her people. She decided to live out her choice of being the "Virgin Queen" who is married to her country and make it publicly visible through the means of fashion.

It was now up to her and her close assistants to develop a specific wardrobe, which would signal her chaste life-style to the people she ruled. During the era, there was an implicit language of colours, accessories and the fabrics, which were read like words. For example, white represented virginity, an embroidered crescent moon meant chastity (Howley, 2009).

Figure 2.1 'The Ditchley portrait'. A painting of Queen Elizabeth I by Marcus Gheeraerts the Younger, ca. 1592, oil on canvas. The Queen's symbolic sartorial choice represented her virginity. © National Portrait Gallery, London.

From 1566 onwards, the Queen's sartorial choices were political ones. Even her portraits were constructed with great calculation to make sure that no physical flaws were ever revealed whilst paying great attention to the symbolic power of her dress. If her subordinates and her people were to accept that she was married to her country, they literally had to see it to believe it. Any doubts of her political power, ability as a ruler and choice to remain single had to be eliminated. Nevertheless, it remains a mystery until this day whether she really was as chaste or had some "bedfellows", as Dr Anna Whitelock called them (Whitelock, 2013).

It is comparable to today's sartorial choices of women in power such as the wardrobe of Jackie Kennedy, Michelle Obama or Carla Bruni who, although not monarchs or single rulers, did have to use their clothing in order to establish and maintain a political and social stance. Jackie Kennedy, for example, employed Oleg Cassini, a Russian aristocrat who had fled from the Russian revolution to the USA. The husband of Hollywood beauty Gene Tierney, Cassini created Dior-like couture costumes for Jackie and made her look feminine, effortlessly chic and beautiful as America's first lady. She had to be perfectly dressed for her role and Cassini was highly experienced in exactly that: He had already dressed many Hollywood leading ladies as a film studio costumier.

Across the Channel and nearly two centuries after Elizabeth I, in France, during the French Revolution, which lasted from 1789 to 1799, pamphlets, music, plays, art and festivals were used to spread revolutionary thoughts and convince the masses to join in. Then, once Napoleon took control over the country, he too used similar propaganda material to secure his role as the Emperor by adding new national holidays (such as his birthday), and organizing fireworks, parades and public balls. He too, had portraits painted of the image he wanted to instil: a military leader, the emperor (Cull, 2003).

In fact, you could easily call these political figures "opinion leaders" – a term which we know in the context of popular culture today and which is discussed in Chapter 5.

When exactly did Propaganda get its new name of "Public Relations"?

To answer this question, one has to look at Edward Bernays, an important shaper of modern-day PR and advertising. He is often called the father of PR or "Spin" or the inventor of PR and other times credited as the father of advertising.

In fact, it can be said that he used both communication instruments. Bernays, who was Sigmund Freud's nephew, closely worked with his uncle's theories on psychology. However, his goal was not to help unlock the inner self of the

Figure 2.2 Model with cigarette holder. Fuselage Fashion Couture show in London, 2002, presenting a collection inspired by the fashion of the 1920s to 1940s and the aesthetic of women smoking at that time. Author's own design, photography and styling.

people but instead by knowing human psychology he wanted to influence and unleash secret desires to manipulate them. He created full campaigns to sell cigarettes to women, bacon to the USA, war to countries and much more as he was hired by banks, corporations and governments. Without his ingenious advertising and PR inventions, such as the testimonial, there would not be the type of advertising we know today. He called his activities "propaganda" but changed it to "public relations" once the former term had been hijacked and gravely misused by the Nazis of WWII.

Case example: Torches of Freedom

Edward Bernays also worked with fashion, as early as in the 1920s. One of his significant media stunts was the "Torches of Freedom" campaign. Among his clients, which included companies, corporations, politicians and the US government, was the tobacco producer Great American Tobacco of Lucky Strike cigarettes. The brief was to raise the female consumers' cigarette consumption. But in the early twentieth century, smoking was considered unthinkable for women, especially in public. Bernays contrived a publicity stunt: He summoned famous and well-regarded women to march down central New York during the 1929 Easter Sunday parade with a lit cigarette in hand. He also summoned journalists to the site so that they could report on the event. No one knew that the parade was not initiated by women who were demonstrating for freedom, but by a tobacco company (Amosa, 2002).

A lot of money had been spent to advertise the 1920s green package of Lucky Strikes and Bernays' goal was to make this colour fashionable, too. Turning to fashion, Bernays organized the "Green Ball" at the Waldorf-Astoria which was attended by leading debutantes of New York. The colour green would be the ball's motif and everyone attending would be required to wear the colour from head to toe: green ball-gowns, green shoes, green gloves, green handkerchiefs, green jewellery (Tye, 2002, p. 39).

To ensure the effective spreading of the message, fashion editors were invited for a Green Fashions Fall Luncheon to dine on green menus. Consequently, and as planned, after the ball magazines such as *Vogue* praised both the colour green and the event itself.

This green fashion craze initiated by Bernays for Lucky Strikes made other tobacco brands uncomfortable, so much so that even the rival tobacco company Camel produced an advertisement depicting a girl wearing a green dress.

A large amount of press coverage was generated by the "Torches of Freedom" campaign and the season's most popular colour, yet the public did not question any of it or considered that the news was artificially staged. The authors of *Propaganda and Mass Persuasion* insist that even today, "propagandists will continue to invent stories about adversaries, falsify statistics, and 'create' news. From the propagandist's point of view, lies must only be told about unverifiable facts" (Cull, 2003).

Bernays had more involvement with the fashion industry, which fascinated him. He found fashion PR to be extremely powerful and exemplary in what propaganda can do, such as make women change their hair styles or opt for a completely different look. According to Véronique Pouillard (2013), Bernays wrote about his fascination of fashion in 1928 in his book *Propaganda* and did not make a distinction between using the word "PR" or "Propaganda" as this was interchangeable at that time.

Bernays worked with fashion on numerous occasions, including in the 1920s when he was hired by French couturier Charles Frederick Worth to help combat the downturn of French fashion at that time and promote it in America (Pouillard, 2013).

Brand communication

Since the advent of PR during the early twentieth century, PR has been the tool which fashion brands use to communicate with a wide audience of their stakeholders. In the diagram below you can see the two-way communication between a fashion brand and the public. The public can be divided into three groups of people:

- The media people, including fashion journalists and editors, bloggers and celebrities who can often be opinion leaders (or influencers) and shape the public's attitudes.
- The public, including all people who might be reached by the brand's communication activities, be it existing customers, potential customers or those who will not buy the brand but might talk about it.
- The industry, which simply put everyone behind the scenes of a brand. Those people will be stakeholders with an interest or investment in the brand such as suppliers and manufacturers, retailers and shareholders. Governments of countries where clothing is produced or where it is sold will have a relationship with the brand, starting from the taxes that need to be paid or production standards that are set in place for the workers. Trade organizations form an important part of a fashion brand's business practices.

There is a direct connection of those three main groups, which the fashion brand interacts with, and the interaction goes both ways. Media people will react to news from the brand and so will the public. The public will hear about a brand's development from different sources, including the media. As an example, when Tom Ford decided to replace his catwalk show with a fashion film in 2015, consumers found out about this from the brand as well as from publications who wrote about it. The consumers can have a positive or negative attitude towards the brand and media communication which feeds right back

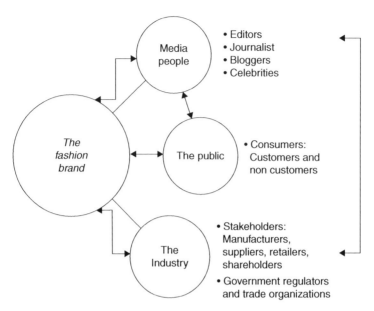

Figure 2.3 Connections between the fashion brand and the public. Author's original illustration.

to both. However, the general public rarely has any communication with the professional industry.

Understanding the core differences between advertising and PR

The Public Relations Society of America defines public relations as: "Public relations is a strategic communication process that builds mutually beneficial relationships between organizations and their publics" (PRSA, 2016).

In contrast, here is the definition of advertising by marketing-guru Philp Kotler (2009): "Advertising is any paid form of non-personal presentation & promotion of ideas, goods, or services by an identified sponsor". In simple words, "Advertising is a means of informing and communicating essential information".

Yet again Kleppners Advertising Procedure states: "Advertising consists of paid notices from identified sponsors normally offered through communication media" (Lane, 2008).

Both have similarities and both are designed to work together, supporting all communication efforts of the brand and usually a brand will try to coordinate

Table 2.1 The main differences between advertising and PR

	Advertising	Public Relations
Frequency of single campaign	Repeated as often as necessary	Works only once
Cost intensity	Very cost intensive	Variable from low to high cost intensity
Control over final outcome	Complete control	Little control if working with journalist
Goal of campaign	Increase sales and revenue	Improve reputation, awareness
Reaction of consumers	Mistrust ads	Trust PR
Marketing goal	Influence opinions and reactions	Influence opinions and reactions

advertising and public relations activities within their communications strategy and of course, the entire Marketing Mix.

Even though advertising and PR works best in combination and sometimes shares a campaign, there may be some basic differences in terms of frequency, cost, control and the reaction of the consumers.

The marketing goals of promotion can have many goals, which are the increase of sales and revenue, image adjustment, or increase of awareness and public acceptance and are usually shared between PR and advertising.

Table 2.1 shows the main differences of advertising and PR.

In terms of the frequency of a campaign, the clear difference is that in advertising, an ad campaign can be shown as often as necessary through the various media channels. However, with PR activities, a journalist might write a single feature in a magazine for the current issue and the same article will not reappear again. The same goes for an event such as a product launch or a fashion show which is only staged once and reported on around the time of it taking place.

The cost intensity is still very high for advertising with one page of a four-colour ad in *Vogue* costing around $200,000. However, in public relations it is possible to use low cost measures such as digital press releases or invite the press to the premises of the PR company and its showrooms. Of course, events and especially fashion weeks can raise this cost which gives PR a wider range in terms of cost intensity than advertising.

In advertising, there is a lot of control over the final outcome of a campaign. From the idea and the design of an ad for example, to the decision of where it will be shown and for how long – all this is determined by a brand. But with public relations, a large part of work for the PR professional means liaising with journalists, bloggers and opinion leaders from the industry with the hope that they will feature the brand in an editorial piece or on their media channel. It is usually impossible to completely control the outcome.

Normally, the goal of the advertising campaign is primarily to increase sales and revenue. Public relations is more concerned with raising awareness of the existence of a brand or product, improving its reputation and acceptance. Ultimately, this is meant to help the brand to grow better in the marketplace and of course, achieve more sales.

Because the customer is aware that with advertising the brand is directly talking to him and trying to sell him something, he is likely to ignore or even mistrust the brand. When PR is used and an industry expert talks about the brand, the customers show much more trust. The downside is that whereas in an ad campaign the brand has complete control over the message, which it is sending to the target customer, it has very little control over say a journalist who is writing about the brand. Overall, advertising can be very costly because any traditional media such as magazines, TV or cinema charge high prices. Public relations can be expensive if it includes an event or show, but usually the expenditure is much lower as no direct media space is purchased.

There is one thing that both advertising and public relations have in common when they promote a brand or product: they want to influence the consumer's opinions and reactions. With both promotional tools the goal is a positive attitude of the consumer towards the brand, the desire to buy it and brand loyalty, which help the overall marketing strategy for the growth, resilience and success of the brand.

Today's fashion brands tend to use both communication tools in their marketing strategy, with a mixture of PR and advertising initiatives such as the use of ads in magazines and simultaneous events which journalists could report on.

But of course, there are also exceptions: Zara is a brand which up to now has hardly ever invested in classic advertising. You will not see any Zara billboards, TV commercials or magazine spreads. For a brand which is known for copying catwalk looks at the speed of light, there is perhaps no need to advertise because this is already done by the high-fashion brands.

A competitor from the same fast fashion segment who does rely on advertising heavily is H&M. Their campaigns are often seen in the city landscape and can feature celebrities.

The role of PR and how it complements advertising

For fashion brands, public relations might work closely with fashion magazines on behalf of a fashion brand.

The PR agency might be a separate department within the fashion brand's headquarters. But this in-house agency will work with smaller local agencies which are knowledgeable about the local market.

Independent PR agencies will take on a number of clients, be their sole PR agent or – as in the example above – be an additional PR agent and form a network and cluster of agencies that their client – the fashion brand – works with.

One might wonder if it is not sufficient for a brand to simply purchase advertising space in the glossy fashion magazines and guarantee sales. However, just as advertising plays a huge role in the Marketing Mix of a brand, it is equally important for brands (some might argue that it is imperative) to be mentioned by an editor of the same fashion magazine in an editorial piece. This is the equivalent of "free advertising" as it is generally much cheaper than if the same page size had been purchased for an ad. For example, one full colour page of advertising in American *Vogue* costs nearly $200,000, but if the editor writes an article the size of the same page, the only cost that the brand has to pay is to the PR agency. The price for the PR work comes at a fraction of the cost of a print ad.

Furthermore, because readers tend to trust PR more than open advertisements, this can be very important for shaping a positive relationship with a brand's audience. This makes the job of public relations professionals quite challenging because liaising with fashion magazines or opinion leaders such as bloggers does not necessarily guarantee a story.

However, there is an unspoken rule that most magazines do give some "editorial" love to clients who have purchased several pages of advertising. If you look through a *Vogue, Elle, Cosmo* or *Harpers Bazaar* and see which fashion brands are featured on the back cover, first pages and fold-outs, you will most likely find their products mentioned in an editorial within the same magazine. In this case, if the PR agency is working for a brand which also purchases advertising, they will have a much easier job of securing press coverage in the issue.

The power of the press is quite substantial: A brand might invest a lot of money in advertising, but when Anna Wintour, Suzy Menkes, Hillary Alexander or Emmanuelle Alt mention a fashion label, it can catapult it into stardom. For the PR professional it is thus highly important to know the editors and journalists of each publication that they would like to work with and approach them accordingly. They also have to genuinely understand the brand which they are working for and find suitable media.

In addition to that, today's influencers (or opinion leaders), such as bloggers and stylists, are just as important as the classic journalists even though there are many discussions on whether opinion leaders can be considered journalists in a classic sense of the word. This is because journalism is supposed to report independently and not be biased by and brand affiliations. However, it is well known that influencers such as bloggers will report on products which they were gifted or paid for, so much so, that blogging has developed into a new profession and pays to make a decent living.

Press pack and press release

When a PR company is looking to get a brand into some glossy fashion magazines, to get journalists talking or the media reporting – both print and digital – it will prepare and send out press kits – a physical or digital compilation of the most important information on the fashion brand, including the latest press releases, photographs of the collection (called look books) and information on the season's inspiration. A press kit might also contain background information on the brand, market data, videos or links to downloadable material and of course small gifts and trinkets.

An important element of the press kit is the press release. A press release is usually a short written text which states the most important information about an event or newsworthy story but is written in an inspiring way which captures the reader's attention. Sometimes the press release is called a press statement, media release or news release. It can have any length ranging from just 300 words to 1000. It can be part of the press kit or it can be sent on its own if it is noteworthy.

The information contained in the press release should be built like a pyramid with the most important and shot sentences at the top, descending to more text throughout the body of the entire press release and allowing for larger sections of text further down on the page.

1. The very first paragraph must provide answers to the five W questions:
   Who? Who are the key players – your company, anyone else involved with the product? Who does your news affect/who does it benefit?
   What? What is the news?
   Why? Why is this happening and why should the reader care?
   Where? Where did this happen or will happen?
   When? Is there a precise timing or time-frame?
   The 5 W might be accompanied by the "H" for how. How did this come about?
2. The second section gives more details on the elements mentioned in the first paragraph. It still has to be concise and to the point.
3. Further down the next section can give details on the brand, its background or history, statistics and an interesting story that supports the main message of the release.
4. Any other details, information or text can be written here but should not contain vital facts of high importance as they might get omitted by the reader. The most important information goes to the top of the pyramid.

Finally, the press release should state the media contacts with instructions on how to contact the PR agent or PR department of the fashion brand for further information. If the press release is not part of a press kit, then it is good to indicate that further media and look books can be obtained in physical or digital format upon request or through a link.

In Figure 2.5, you can see examples of two physical look books by Hugo Boss with one for the BOSS Men's Collection of Fall/Winter 2016 and the other of Boss Women's Collection Fall/Winter 2016. The spiral-bound booklets show images taken directly from the catwalk show for the women's collection and

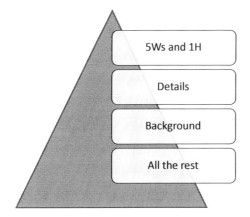

Figure 2.4 The press release pyramid. Author's original illustration.

Figure 2.5 Hugo Boss look books, Fall/Winter 2016 with menswear accessories on the left and a runway shot of womenswear on the right. Image kindly provided by Hugo Boss.

photo stills for the menswear collection. Both booklets include stills of accessories and feature the name and product number of each item. These are handy
for journalists when they want to request more information on the item but are
also designed for buyers who need the product code for orders.

The booklets offer an internet link to the Hugo Boss press service portal
where a trend report and all of the look book pictures can be downloaded for
further use.

Good PR must not only know which journalist might be interested in writing
about which product, they must also know the profiles of the readership. This is
another area where both advertising and PR use the same information.

A professional who is constantly working with the same media will know
these things by heart, but in case the information is not at hand, it can easily be
looked up:

> Every publication usually offers something called "media data" on their
> website. More than the content of the magazine, this is the information
> which is vital for advertising and PR alike. The Media Data will contain
> Rate Cards, or the prices for buying advertising space in the magazine. In
> the case of *Vogue*, one full-colour page costs around $200,000 in the USA.
> There will also be data on the cost of digital advertising space.

Furthermore, there is data on the readership with a look at the lifestyle (or
demographics). This usually includes the average age or age-span of the readers,
whether they are male or female, if they are educated, how much they earn and
what their lifestyle is generally like.

Both advertising and PR must understand what audience they want to communicate with when they launch a campaign. Is their target reader (and thus target
customer) an affluent, urban female in her 30s with a high interest in designer
brands? Or is the reader a teenager who still lives at home and can only buy cheaper
products with their pocket money? Perhaps the target customer is a man who likes
to do sports and nature, and who needs durable and eco-friendly clothing?

Case example: The Lawn Tennis Association targeting a local niche audience

The successful PR agency in London called Exposure PR has worked for
established and well known clients such as Levis, Jaeger, Barbour and
Uniqlo and is responsible for successfully reviving Doc Martens with their
fresh campaigns.

The agency works for large brands with broad target audiences as well as localized and small brands.

You might see this case as a local "grassroots" organization in London, on a very small scale.

In 2004, the Lawn Tennis Association, the national governing body for tennis throughout the UK which also organizes Wimbledon, approached Exposure to help them spread the word about playing tennis to young people in the vicinity. The LTA had only managed to train one tennis star on home turf and wanted to get more young kids to join them.

So how could the agency define the target market of their client? Exposure decided to target the hip and fashion-conscious youths of Greater London, so all those who participate in the buzzing fashion scene of London. Exposer recruited a graduate from the famed Central Saint Martins' University to design an innovative and unusual capsule collection of tennis clothes. The collection was produced and then shot by a professional photographer. The images were published not in high-fashion glossy magazines but in daily and local papers. This is a good example to illustrate that word-of-mouth and PR might be more effective in reaching the target group than pure advertising.

Other activities that PR companies do can include the organization of fashion shows, product launches or shop launches, securing celebrity endorsements, blogger relations and social media projects.

PR can also be quite serious: Strategic and financially-focused PR companies might be in charge of dealing with all the publicity for the financial activities of a company. It is not only large corporations that offer an IPO (Initial Public Offering) and join the stock market, but also fashion companies which are active on the stock exchange such as LVMH, Richemont or Farfetch. PR can help them here as they are obliged to report their financial results and activities at specified intervals. The same can be observed when there are take-overs of businesses or new owners, for example such as the take-over of Valentino by the financial vehicle Mayhoola of the second wife of the former Emir of Qatar, Her Highness Sheikha Mozah bint Nasser Al Missned, in 2013 and the take-over of Balmain in 2016.

Strategic public relations can also deal with crises, when a company is involved in a scandal. A good example is when in 2014, the German clothing brand Tom Tailor was accused of using cat fur for the bobbles of their winter knitted hats, even though they had a no-fur company policy.

In such cases, advertising would not be of much use to shape the public's opinion and PR is the best method to proceed.

Olga Mitterfellner Designs

Figure 2.6 Original drawings, textile designs and the finished hand-made garments on the model showing an innovative tennis collection for the Lawn Tennis Association. Author's original designs, styling and photographs.

Interview with Teresa Havvas on Lipcote

Figure 2.7 Teresa Havvas, image by photographer Julia Sterre Schmitz.

Teresa Havvas is a Lifestyle and Beauty Communication expert and educator, founder of The Advisory Creative Counsel, as well as Head of Brand for Lipcote & Co – Lipcote (iconic lipstick top-coat) and Browcote (brow gel) are award-winning products.

Q: Please tell me about yourself

TH: Entrepreneurial and spirited, I live by a good projects, good people philosophy, and through all campaigns is a thread towards creating stories with cause and purpose at it's heart.

I specialize in fashion, beauty and lifestyle. Have been in industry for over 15 years launching and championing independent and on the rise designers, hair and beauty salons, accessory labels, a style magazine, as well as in house with a global lifestyle brand.

I graduated from LCF class of 2000, in what was then one of the few holistic, BA Fashion Promotion degrees; a course that was innovated by industry's best teaching from the world of PR, marketing, journalism, culture and broadcasting. This is what provided me with the ultimate platform from which to launch my career as a PR professional, with distinctive and intuitive creative potential. Stories that connect, in an authentic, engaging way and build the genuine relationships to make them resonate is what drives me. It's also why I teach with such passion; to give back and inspire responsible creative practice which encourages original thinking.

Q: What inspires you?

TH: Connection. The creative conscious and the progressive ... those who come through to manifest their vision, against the odds, and the grain, cultivating messages that mean something, with social impact and substance that goes beyond the screen. The new creatives I mentor; a mutual alliance where my expertise and their fresh skill set collide to ignite ideas with intention. I'm inspired when my energy for a project ignites a person's inner confidence and belief to be bold.

I welcome the opportunities to collaborate with those open to push parameters so we can free a new perspective and stories that make you feel something.

I surround myself with a lot of creatives, image makers and visual story tellers, who come from all walks and backgrounds, so that I am constantly learning, challenging and being open to create freely – make time for play with those who support you and the people and projects you believe in and magic happens.

Q: Tell me about your Lipcote project

TH: We have just introduced a new framework 'social for social' dedicated to true followers of the brand. A social event, which captures and produces a real time campaign, and subsequent content that continues to tell stories post party, by those who have a genuine relationship with us.

We wanted to push the traditional launch party format to celebrate our new look packs, with an experience that captures community, conversation, self-expression and above all fun – key pillars to the Lipcote and Co brand.

All elements from venue, catering, flowers and pampering partners, to embroidery body confidence workshops and story-telling experiences that link to honest experiences about how we feel about lipstick meant that we were able to bring together an authentic live campaign.

Friends and family of the brand also had an opportunity to meet those behind the brand face to face and learn more about our partnering charity – Get Lippy by Eve Appeal. A studio to capture photos of participating guests from press, bloggers, industry and internal team would become the makings of our campaign. All hosted at the Hunter Collective, an inspired co working salon for enterprising hair and beauty freelancers.

We broke tradition with a day event, held on a Sunday, and was a full house filled with an invite only crowd, we knew would care and resonate.

We explored and embraced what it is to be social in all aspects and took time to acknowledge and celebrate brand to people relationships, which will be remembered for the right reasons. With the landscape operating at such a fast pace, sometimes the most brave thing to do, is pause, audit and reaffirm intention so that you can move forward to create customer journeys and experiences that connect in a more human way.

Q: How did you understand the audience?

TH: Research and development are vital, and with us, it's hands on and approached responsibly. I have spent years seeking out the true fans of our brand – make up artists, beauty journalists, industry experts and those who buy us, which I would often connect with at public beauty and fashion related events and festivals.

It is a grass roots, effective approach, and a long-term process, which you need to keep working on and we look at all media channels to listen and learn.

I put myself out there to meet as many people as possible, to discover as much as possible about them from a mind set and ethnographic point of view, so that understanding can inspire new ways to reach them with messages that are relevant.

I work with insights and forecasting professionals and apply resources, collaborate with select creative and media teams and beauty bodies and category managers/ buyers to validate and challenge thinking, so that I stay current. My teaching also enables me to focus group new ideas and set live project briefs, so that young creatives and illustrators have an opportunity to work with us on projects.

It's a great deal of team work with great teams all on board because they too believe in the brand.

Q: How did you go about setting your goals and achieving them?

TH: Goals are set as series of mini campaigns that we roll out throughout the year, aligned to key retailer partners and collaborators, each with a message that supports our values.

We forward plan as much as possible, and from a commercial perspective, we focus on a balance of trade and consumer integrated strategies within manageable set budgets.

Figure 2.8 Lipcote lipstick sealer. With kind permission by Teresa Havvas and Lipcote.

We achieve by doing, and learning from what worked/did not work to keep getting better.

Q: What were the limitations?

TH: There are no limits as such, only the usual budget constraints, which means that we need to allow for a longer time frame to reach our potential and the time to negotiate the partnerships, so that they are mutually beneficial.

Money in my opinion accelerates the process. For as long as we keep engaging and giving our customers the product they want with values they care about, we have time.

When you work with any brand, big or small, Process is integral to reaching your aspirations. As a creative individual, this, over the years, has been the hardest to grasp and master … it may well be the most important P in the mix.

Q: Do you see a link of PR and advertising working together?

TH: Yes, I think that it's circular, one feeds the other. I believe that the best PRs think like advertisers and that the best in advertising thinks as a PR. It's all campaigns and it takes a holistic approach with above and below the line blending to form a cohesive interface that consumers will engage with.

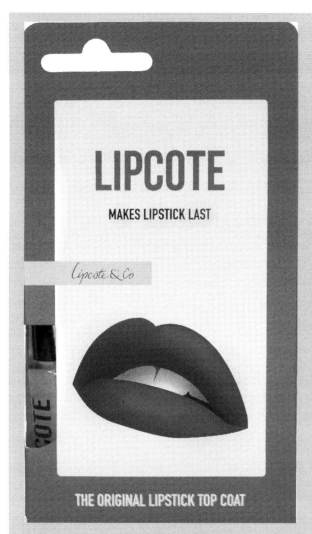

Figure 2.9 Lipcote packaging. With kind permission by
Teresa Havvas and Lipcote.

Q: How do you see ethics and social responsibility when working in
PR? And what about beauty standards?

TH: It's fundamental that practitioners also give time to educate and
create platforms that seek out talent to nurture and guide future
communicators. I feel that all campaigns should consider positive
social impact – a cause to pioneer so that the power goes further with
intention, integrity and above all transparency. PR when delivered
well can drive change and inspire original thinking.

Figure 2.10 Lipcote product display. With kind permission by Teresa Havvas and Lipcote.

Beauty standards are high, and rightfully so, we are governed with a spot light on calling out the bluffers so that the future feels brighter for the experts and the accredited, to reign strong again.

I'm of the thinking that follower numbers do not act a barometer for success, success comes with delivering with substance and collaboration with those who are experienced, knowledgeable and informed.

Social media acts as a listening tool to understand, and we must apply it with care to create.

Q: What are your recommendations for current and future PR professionals?

TH: To honour your creative spirit. Research and explore, be curious and challenge; respectfully disrupt and build campaigns with heart, with those who share your thinking and push you to reach your potential so that we can keep original thought thriving. Remember the R in PR is Relationships; *feel, connect and make them responsibly.*

Ethical considerations

Public relations is an evolvement of propaganda and is nearly identical in its content. The only difference is the name. Whatever term you use to describe it, it has the power and the goal to actively manipulate the mind of masses of people to the advantage of a particular brand, person or organization. The relationship between the two is often one-sided and only benefits one party. We are now at an age where PR has evolved so much that there are trusted practices of the profession and measurable outcomes, making it a lucrative instrument for any fashion brand.

Furthermore, PR stunts are often disguised as a real social occurrence, such as in the example of the "Torches of Freedom" by Bernays. This means that the consumers are fooled and cannot make an informed decision about a particular product or a brand. The art of PR includes understanding the psychology of individuals and the masses and using the most suitable mass media instruments to influence if not control society.

It is imperative to consider the ethical implications of any such action, especially when negative, unhealthy or unfair things are falsely portrayed as something positive, such as has been done with portraying cigarettes as healthy and highly fashionable.

Further reading

Bernays, E. and Miller, M. C. (2004) *Propaganda*. New York: Ig Publishing.

Chomsky, N. (1995) *Manufacturing Consent: The Political Economy of the Mass Media*. London: Vintage.

Cope, J. and Maloney, D. (2016) *Fashion Promotion in Practice*. London: Bloomsbury.

Dowson, R. and Bassett, D. (2018) *Event Planning and Management: A Practical Handbook for PR and Events Professionals*. London: Kogan Page.

Diamond, J. (2015) *Retail Advertising and Promotion*. New York: Fairchild.

Moore, G. (2012) *Basics Fashion Management: Fashion Promotion 02: Fashion Promotion: Building a Brand through Marketing and Communication*. Lausanne, Switzerland: Bloomsbury Publishing PLC; Imprint: AVA Publishing SA.

Perlman, S. and Sherman, G. J. (2012) *Fashion Public Relations*. New York: Fairchild.

Smith, P. R. and Zook, Z. (2016) *Marketing Communications: Offline and Online Integration, Engagement and Analytics*. 6th edn. London: Kogan Page.

Tye, L. (2002) *The Father of Spin: Edward L. Bernays and the Birth of Public Relations*. New York: Henry Holt (Owl Books).

The Marketing Mix and communications tools

3

Chapter topics

The original Marketing Mix

As demonstrated in the previous chapters, some of the important people who developed the foundation of modern-day marketing, advertising and PR were: Neil H. Borden and E. Jerome McCarthy, Edward Bernays, Ernest Dichter, Ivy Lee, Elmo Lewis, Walter Dill Scott and Abraham Maslow.

It was during the active years of Edward Bernays, once the term "Public Relations" had been established, that a further new marketing term emerged. The "Marketing Mix" was invented by one of the many famous thinkers of the twentieth century, Neil Borden, who contrived the Marketing Mix in 1940, and which went on to become a significant foundation of former and current marketing theories as well as a widespread framework used in higher education for marketing.

The mix includes all the important basic elements that need to be in place and in harmony in order to make a brand successful as well as profitable. In 1960, E. Jerome McCarthy took the theory a step further and segmented those elements into separate groups, called the 4Ps:

Product
Price
Place
Promotion

The 4 basic Ps determine the product which needs to be produced and distributed, the place where it is on offer, its price and its promotion through communication strategies such as advertising and public relations. In theory, the Ps can be controlled and used to ensure that the business is profitable.

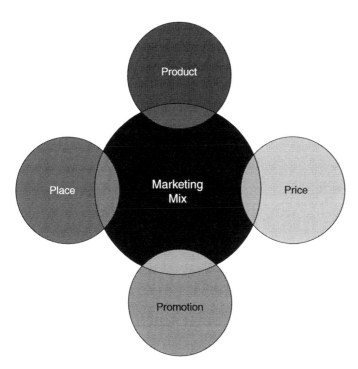

Figure 3.1 The Marketing Mix. Author's original illustration based on the original Marketing Mix.

The 4Ps in detail

> Product
> Price
> Place
> Promotion

Plus 3: Process, Physical Evidence, People

In the 1980s, the four Marketing Mix Ps were expanded further to 7Ps, and had more of a focus on services which included process (service process), physical evidence and people (participants) (Kotler *et al.* 2009, p.17).

Much literature and consequent discussions refer to the 4, 7, 8 or more Ps with various adaptations and expansions. This chapter looks at the classical 4Ps in depth and looks at the additional 3 which Booms and Bitner proposed in 1981.

Product

The product is arguably a key component of the Marketing Mix and most important to any fashion business which sells tangible and physical products, such as clothing, shoes, accessories etc. This might also include perfume, cosmetics, jewellery and watches. Some fashion brands consciously opt for a so-called brand-extension or brand-stretches into other segments, meaning that they might also offer travel experiences such as hotels, restaurants, food, homeware, flowers and others.

A prime example is Armani which offers several fashion brands and all the items listed above, at various price points from luxury to affordable luxury and premium prices.

Zara is another brand whose focus is on the clothing segment, but who also has the Zara Home stores, separated from their fashion stores, offering homeware ranges and a selection of clothing in the fast-fashion price range.

An important part of making a fashion product desirable for consumers is branding.

A brand, according to Kotler is "a name, term, sign, symbol, design or a combination of these, that identifies the maker or seller of the product or service" (Kotler *et al.* 2009, p.511).

As mentioned in Chapter 1, brands became prevalent with the onset of the industrial revolution to better distinguish products from various manufacturers and branding has grown into an art and profession of its own over the last centuries. The brand name, logo and features are an integral part of it – it makes up a fashion brand's reputation regarding quality and performance. The packaging of a brand might also add to the way consumers perceive and enjoy a brand.

Table 3.1 The 7 Ps. Based on Kotler et al. (2009).

Product/Service	Price	Promotion	Place	Physical evidence	Process	People
Product or service	Regular price	Advertising	Global channels	Tangible service environment and evidence	Service design	Staff
Design features	Discount price	Public relations	Assortments		Self-service technologies	Customers
Brand name	Payment conditions	Sales promotion	Locations	Sound		
Packaging	Pricing strategies	Direct marketing	Inventory	Sight		
Services		Online and offline	Transport	Smell		
				Taste		
				Touch		
				Packaging		

For fashion consumers, the brand's image can sometimes overshadow the product itself and give way to accepting hefty prices. Brands like Supreme have been changing the way luxury fashion is perceived and purchased in the last years when the streetwear brand teamed up with luxury fashion. The association with Supreme led to customers anticipating a so-called "product drop" for weeks in advance, later queuing up at the stores and hoping to get a product before it is "sold out". The quality of the product was hardly in the forefront of their minds as they did not get to test and inspect it prior to purchasing. The affiliation of the brands was enough to cause a hype.

The fashion product can also be complemented by a service or experience, such as a beauty treatment, an app, or an event, but is ultimately tied to the fashion brand and the core product that it is known for. For businesses that have a focus on service, the supplemental 3Ps (as described further on in this chapter) are an essential element of their Marketing Mix.

Price

The pricing strategy of a fashion business determines how much customers have to pay in order to receive the goods or services. Most times, the price is directly connected to the market level, the quality and possibly reputation with haute couture being highly expensive and fast fashion (or throwaway fashion) being most affordable.

The various price levels of a fashion product can be categorized within a hierarchy of price and quality in the pyramid shown in Figure 3.2.

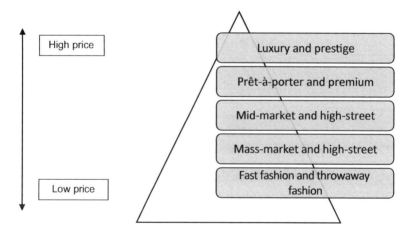

Figure 3.2 Hierarchy of price and quality pyramid. Author's original illustration.

The price is determined by the production and distribution costs, as well as the mark up that the brand can achieve. A mass-produced item might have a low mark up but the business remains profitable due to the sheer volume of items sold. A hand-crafted luxury piece such as a watch might be of limited production numbers and would need a high mark up and price to justify the reduced quantity made as well as the time, effort and materials that are used in its manufacture.

A brand also has to monitor competitors' pricing carefully, understand what the customer is prepared to pay and whether he or she will return for repeat purchases.

In terms of product promotion, pricing can be used by means of discounts, deals (i.e. buy one get one 50% off) or vouchers in order to entice the customer to make a purchase.

Place

This P is predominantly involved in the transport, logistics and distribution of fashion through various sales channels. Enough merchandise must be produced or sourced so it can be offered at the "place" which can be on-line, off-line, through mail-order catalogues or even directly from the manufacturer. The brand must ensure the correct assortment and carefully monitor its inventory. Furthermore, in a very globalized business, the place is no longer necessarily fixed to one place of origin and local distribution. Luxury fashion brands might still produce their products in one atelier, the place where the brand originated many decades ago, but their consumers will expect to purchase the products in a myriad of global locations. The mid-market and fast-fashion brands often produce in several countries and in quantities which need a high level of management. Time management also plays a role as the product must reach the place or be available through any sales channel in the correct quantities.

Furthermore, consumers now want a physical and digital place of purchase to be highly engaging, entertaining and experiential. Chapter 8 takes a closer look at how this can be achieved through sensory branding and digital integration.

Promotion

This P is the focus of this book and it stands for effective communication with the target customer and prospective customer with the goal of increasing awareness, profit or both. Promotion includes advertising and public relations, sales promotion and direct marketing and can be conducted on-line, off-line and in person, through visual merchandizing, celebrity endorsement, sponsorship and through guerrilla marketing.

As mentioned in Chapter 1, the USA was one of the pioneers when it came to post-industrial advertising and the first advertising agencies emerged there in the latter half of the nineteenth century, such as J. Walter Thompson (founded in 1864 and still active today) and N.W. Ayer & Sons.

Promotion is also highly reliant on the mass media landscape such as newspapers, cinema, TV and radio and of course digital media. The choice of promotional channels is part of the communications strategy planning that a business has to establish. This involves setting goals, budgets and measurable Key Performance Indicators (KPIs) to monitor the outcome of the communications endeavours.

Promotion is also a question of cost because campaigns and appropriate channels can be very expensive. Equally, a well-planned and executed promotional activity by a brand can have high return-on-investment. Most brands cannot exist without promotional activities.

Marketing communications tools

The business strategy of any company will likely include overall objectives and the marketing department will make an appropriate marketing plan. This is then transferred onto an operational plan which describes how marketing communications should be executed.

The marketing communications plan will make a time-frame in which the most appropriate tools will be implemented and how. In terms of the Marketing Mix, it is the P for Promotion.

Figure 3.3 shows an approach to the Integrated Marketing Communications plan and the various tools available. Depending on the business needs, this can be reduced, expanded or changed to best fit the strategic and marketing goals and usually a combination of on-line and off-line measures is used, which can be classified into Above-the-Line and Below-the-Line activities. These are explained in more detail in Chapter 4 and consist of:

- Public Relations
- Advertising
- Social media activities (across various platforms and in collaboration with social media personalities)
- Tradeshows, conferences, presentations and events
- Sales promotions (direct mail, in store or on-line)

In order to choose the appropriate tools, it is important to understand whether the fashion brand wants to use mass communication (mass marketing) or very targeted communication (target marketing).

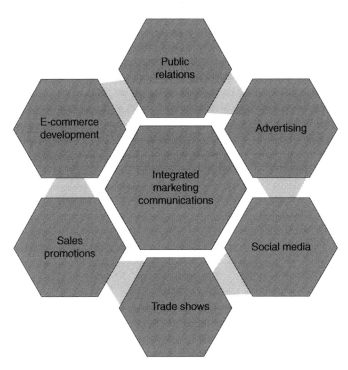

Figure 3.3 Integrated Marketing Communications. Author's original illustration.

Mass marketing

Mass marketing is intended to appeal to all, with no specific target market in mind.

This can work especially well with staple products such as basic socks, basic underwear, the cotton T-shirt because – one might argue – everyone will need these items in their lives, no matter who they are.

In this case, to boost a bland staple product, differentiate the brand from its competitors and reach a mass market, collaborations between brands can be very useful, as was done in the case of H&M who collaborated with David Beckham for their underwear.

NB: Above-the-line communication is most suitable for mass marketing.

Target marketing

With target marketing you spend time (and money) researching your customer.

The advantage here is that from then on your marketing efforts are streamlined and efficient – you can reach the people who will actually spend money on your brand.

The brand communications plan will be tailored to address these specific customers.

NB: Below-the-line communication is most suitable for target marketing.

The supplemental 3Ps

People

People are those who are directly and indirectly connected to the consumer and play a role in the product or service that is offered. Those people might be involved in the design, production and distribution or delivery of the product. They might be sales assistants or customer service employees online and offline.

In terms of customer service, this is a pivotal contact point and businesses must take this very seriously to achieve a positive and lasting relationship with the consumer as well as repeat sales. A prime example comes from the aviation industry where airlines compete for the passengers. No matter what the booking process and pre-flight process experience was, the ultimate test is the flight itself. The cabin crew and flight crew represent everything the airline stands for, in a confined space, within a limited amount of time and with a pre-determined selection of service items for the passenger. Their service, appearance and competence often determine whether a passenger will choose the same airline for their next flight or not.

It is the same for fashion brands where the sales assistants only have a limited amount of time to really impress the customer and make him or her return next time. In addition, and contrary to aviation, the product might not have been purchased yet and it is up to the staff to entice the consumer to buy.

Furthermore, there is the management and marketing personnel within the business which plays a significant role behind the scenes of a brand but with a powerful effect on consumers. As the case example at the end of this chapter shows, unethical or unwise behaviour can actively disappoint customers and cause a brand to decline.

Process

The word process can be substituted by the word system. This is the system any and every business needs to have in order to thrive because it is responsible for delivering a service to the customer. It might be the technological processes which would include the process of manufacturing goods and adapting them for the needs of clients as well as suppy chain management (SCM). (digitalerra, 2016), the electronic process or a transaction process (payment systems), aftersales process, as well as all elements of the customer journey.

A prime example of "process" in place is the subscription business trend in fashion and especially in beauty and cosmetics. Birchbox is one company which offers a seamless customer journey from signing up online to receiving regular product deliveries and customizing the subscription. The brand can only do well if its process is completely thought through.

Physical evidence

These are tangible elements of the brand where the customer experiences the service or receives evidence of the brand's ethos. For example, the tangible elements within the service environment, these might be the building or store, the sound, sight, smell, taste and touch within those premises, as well as any material cues. Brochures, flyers, business cards or a website could be considered as the service environment and its evidence. Physical evidence is therefore connected to the P for Place and elements of this have been extracted and separated out as "physical evidence".

Further elements of this evidence can be packaging, such as the shopping bags and wrapping paper and tags and labels on the garments. If one buys a luxury item, careful packaging in quality material is expected, whereas a fast fashion store might ask the customer to pay extra for a plastic bag.

The brochure by a watchmaker or jewellery brand might be printed on glossy, good quality paper and this again will signal the brand's positioning, identity and market level to the consumer.

Overall, the physical evidence has to show consistency not only with one retail place but across all stores and even online.

According to the Oxford College of Marketing (2013), the staff have to look smart and tidy and be dressed appropriately and might benefit from wearing uniforms or adhering to a dress policy that leads to a consistent image for existing and potential customers.

The New Marketing Mix: 4Ds replace the 4Ps

The twenty-first century calls for a New Marketing Mix and, due to global changes, it is questionable whether the old Marketing Mix would still be relevant to all types of fashion businesses.

Arguably, a New Marketing Mix would be useful where the 4Ps are replaced by 4Ds.

What are those 4Ds?

Diversity replacing place: Companies need to think globally, because they are trading to diverse regions and cultures. China and India are set to supersede the American market in the near future (Euromonitor) so all companies should consider how they could sell to new markets and hire knowledgeable staff. The marketplace is now virtually everywhere and anywhere, very diverse and international.

Even in the home country, increasingly, fashion consumers want to see their own diversity respected and reflected in the way brands communicate with them. The UK's *Vogue* magazine has, for example, changed its editorial team to include a broader spectrum of races and ethnicities in their staff, which is a step that was much celebrated within the fashion industry. The UK is a highly diverse country, London in particular, so it is no longer possible to ignore this fact at a fashion publication.

Digitalization replacing promotion: All digital channels are important and this is where a brand's promotion takes place. When you add digital technology in a bricks-and-mortar store, like Burberry did, you can use it to promote your product at the POS. Fashion brands have to engage with consumers through different devices and platforms, specifically tailored to the habitual communication channels of the age group and location. Even if a promotional activity is in-store or a guerrilla marketing style installation, it should still be supported by digital activities.

Design replacing product: There are new technologies revolutionizing the way we design products. Nanotechnology, smart textiles and 3D or 4D printing is going to change the product from conception to production. Brands like Chanel have incorporated 3D printed textiles into their high-end collections, whilst fast-fashion brand Uniqlo is well known for their Heat Tech and Airism fabrics with smart properties.

Furthermore, trends are changing rapidly now with very few brands still adhering to around two collections per year, as was the norm only a few decades ago. As brands "drop" (or release) collections frequently, consumers pay more attention to the design and style of the product. It has to be trendy and interesting for a brand to make a sale and design is the key to this.

Desire replacing price: With neuroscience revealing mysteries of the consumer's brain, science and marketing realize what makes people tick. Although price is still important, more important is the creation of desire within the consumer's mind. If a brand has a great story, promotes itself through the right channels

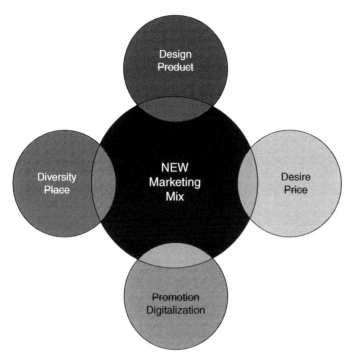

Figure 3.4 The New Marketing Mix: 4Ds. Author's original illustration.

and creates products and a brand identity which is unique, the consumer will long for this brand and agree to the price. It is said that the new great consumer group called Generation Y (or Millennials) is more concerned with a brand's image than the price or even the quality. But how about Generation Z and Alpha who follow on? It is imperative for fashion brands to understand how to tap into the emotion of desire with all young generations whilst not alienating the older ones.

Interview with Sharon Hughes on Donna Sharp

Sharon Hughes is an internationally recognized speaker, fashion marketing professional and educator specializing in digital and social media strategy for fashion business. She also excels in corporate collaboration, curriculum development and student experience. Sharon has worked in marketing management for brands such as Macy's Inc, InStyle Magazine UK, Lori's Shoes, Limited Brands and Chanel.com.

Figure 3.5 Sharon Hughes.

Sharon completed her BS degree in Marketing Management and Fashion Merchandising, Eastern Kentucky University (USA) and postgraduate study in International Marketing at the London Metropolitan University (LMU), her MA research was conducted in Personal Branding and by way of an interview for this research with the editor, she was hired at InStyle Magazine UK. In 2008, she took on a role as Online Marketing Manager for a globally renowned shoe store, Lori's Shoes; due to the lack of resources for digital marketers at that time, she was inspired to create the Online Marketing and Social Media short course for LCF, where she is still a frequent guest lecturer.

Sharon is also the founder of a budding creative arts education initiative and former fashion and lifestyle writer for *Career Girl Daily*. She's been published in *Arts Professional* magazine, *Stylist* and Dubai's *What's*

Figure 3.6 New brand imagery for the Donna Sharp brand. With kind permission by Sharon Hughes.

On magazine. Originally from Louisville, KY, she has lived in four countries and various cities in the US and is effortlessly leaving her mark around the globe.

Q: What does marketing mean to you?

SH: Marketing means to me presenting the right product, at the right price, to the right target audience, and in the right place. It is about establishing relationships with consumers by appealing to their lifestyle and maintaining those relationships by understanding their needs and wants as they progress through life.

Q: Please tell me about the project you did for the Donna Sharp Brand. How did you use the principles of marketing for it?

SH: As Director of Marketing for American Heritage Textiles (a bedding brand), I've been charged with rebranding a new company with an old but well-established 90s brand, Donna Sharp. Changing mindsets of people who are very loyal to a former company is very challenging, I would say the most challenging element of my role.

But as the new owner took over Donna Sharp [the company], it was set to change as the Donna Sharp, the brand. With establishing a new mission and brand values I took the Head of Departments, our CEO and Owner through strategic branding seminars in which I used the 4Ps to discuss our new plans. From redefining our product (who is the Donna Sharp Brand, what do we stand for, who do we create products for – our customers), our pricing strategy was reestablished for there wasn't one prior to my entry, therefore, as you can see from the chart, products will be launched within four pricing and positioning ranges, as well as priced and launched accordingly throughout the seasons. Our collections (via e-commerce) will be launched sporadically throughout the year, this will keep our e-commerce as fresh as possible. Feeding the current drive of online shoppers, for studies show consumers shop more often and have a desire for new arrivals and sales as they enter e-commerce sites.

As a manufacturer and retailer, we had to establish our place in the market, for not only do we sell on our own website, but we sell on partner websites such as Wayfair, along with wholesale clients such as boutique shops and catalogue sites.

Regarding promotions, previously Donna Sharp's promotional material has been quite bland, uninviting and confusing. The campaigns prior to my arrival featured models aged in their 20s when Donna Sharp's youngest consumer is in their 50s. Therefore, the face of the brand was not representative of the shareholders of the brand. Therefore, for our spring campaigns we launched an integrated strategy utilizing print and digital mediums, website, PPC and social media. We chose models that were aged appropriately to our existing and aspirational customer and was much more diverse. With $1.2 trillion in spending power, African-American consumers are an important population for smart brands that want to grow market share and brand preference. Therefore, you can see the results of this campaign attached. Our marketing materials and promotions are looking cleaner, sharper and more approachable. Most importantly, up-to-date, current and diverse. [Sharon modelled herself in the campaign to represent diversity.]

Q: Do you think that you used all seven Ps and if so, how did you use them?

SH: Eventually yes. People, process and physical evidence have fallen in line with how we position our parent company to our existing customers as they age, maintain relationships they set for their children, Gen X and establish products, price and diverse promotions that will attract new customers (older Millennials).

Q: Did you use any marketing and branding communications tools?

SH: Yes.

Q: What was the outcome of the project?

SH: Still ongoing. However, our sales have increased by 21 per cent. Website traffic has increased by 53 per cent. Our social media engagement has increased. Our review average is 4.7 out of 5.0 and we have launched a modern brand called Your Lifestyles to service the new customer we wish to attract. Therefore, I would say we are moving in the right direction.

Q: Did anything surprise you?

SH: Yes, how challenging it is to train internal teams to new brand standards and how loyal customers over 55 really are.

Figure 3.7 New brand imagery for Donna Sharp. With kind permission by Sharon Hughes.

Figure 3.8 New brand imagery for Donna Sharp featuring diversity. With kind permission by Sharon Hughes.

Figure 3.9 New product and pricing strategy for Donna Sharp. With kind permission by Sharon Hughes.

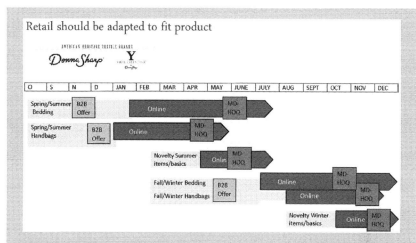

Figure 3.10 Planning of product launch for Donna Sharp. With kind permission by Sharon Hughes.

Ethical considerations

Ethics should be considered with every P of the Marketing Mix.

Product

Is it sustainable or can it be recycled? Is it safe to use for the intended target group, both in a physical and mental sense? In other industries, the impact of an unethical product can be more obvious, such as the marketing of fast food, gambling, alcohol and tobacco. When Abercrombie & Fitch launched their t-shirts with prints that were racist and insulting to Asians and Asian Americans, those individuals joined in protest. The company was unapologetic and reluctantly pulled the products from the shelves, after the negative press became extensive.

Mintel published a study on ethical attitudes in the US in 2015 and found that over 60 per cent of consumers find ethical issues important and 35 per cent of customers will stop purchasing products from brands which they deem unethical. Furthermore, consumers do not feel comfortable when a brand is successful by exploiting someone (Mintel, 2015). This means that ethics are not only a personal issue for a marketing professional but also a strategic issue for a fashion company, possibly causing a decline in revenue when not addressed appropriately.

This is why it is important to ask: How is the product manufactured? Is the supply chain sustainable and does it respect nature, humans and animals along the way? If not, can any of these points be improved?

Promotion

Promotion is a very prominent ethical concern, as it has evolved alongside highly unethical practices. Promotion can often be manipulative, misleading and cause harm to the users. Chapter 9 is dedicated to the harmful side-effects of promotion, especially in advertising.

Place and retail spaces are often full of deceit and manipulation. The prime example is the lure of sales signs into shops where a sale has been pre-calculated and is a trick to get a customer through the door. Online, consumers are often bombarded with messages, targeted advertising and aggressive newsletters which are designed to entice a purchase.

Furthermore, as discussed in Chapter 8, flagship stores, retail buildings and shops can gentrify entire areas, driving out small and diverse businesses and changing the social and urban life for inhabitants.

Price

This leads to the question of price: Consumers are often persuaded to buy now and pay later, pay in instalments or run up their credit cared or store card bill. Whilst paying in instalments can arguably be a great invention and help consumers to buy expensive things which normally they would not be able to afford, the pricing strategies can often leave people in serious debt.

People

Finally, people and the sales force of many fashion brands are trained and forced to behave in an unethical way. Sales staff are trained in techniques of psychological persuasion and consumers often do not realize this. How often is the service provided by a sales assistant the ultimate decision factor? How often do they appear to be as nice as our best friends? Whilst great service is a benefit, a fashion company needs to have clear guidelines on ethical code of practice.

Authors such as Naomi Klein, Jean Kilbourne, Naomi Wolf and organizations such as Adbusters have written about the problems with manipulative, globalized and unethical marketing to adults and children.

Some brands have taken the ethical approach very seriously and tried to implement a best practice initiative at every step of their business. Sadly, there are only a handful of such brands. Brunello Cucinelli, Patagonia, Stella McCartney and People Tree are a rare breed, but luckily brands are realizing that consumers expect some sort of ethics from the brand, which in turns means that the brands need to implement some measures.

Further reading

Easey, M. (2009) *Fashion Marketing*. 3rd edn. Oxford: Blackwell (available as an e-book).

Jackson, T. and Shaw, D. (2009) *Mastering Fashion Marketing*. New York: Palgrave Macmillan.

Jobber, D. (2010) *Principles and Practice of Marketing*. 6th edn. London: McGraw Hill.

Kotler, P., Armstrong, G., Wong, V. and Saunders, J. (2012) *Principles of Marketing*. 5th European edn. Harlow: FT Prentice Hall.

Kotler, P. and Lane Keller, K. (2016) *Marketing Management*. Global Edition, 15th edn. Harlow: Pearson Education Limited.

Creating the marketing message

4

Branding and marketing communications

Chapter topics

The advertising agency

Around the turn of the nineteenth century, the first advertising agencies were formed, which are quite similar to the type of agencies we know today. However, the original advertising agencies usually provided a fraction of the services that are on offer now. In the 1980s when small agencies merged with others and became large networks, they were able to operate on a worldwide scale. This is highly relevant in today's business world, which is mostly global. With a global market place, agencies have also seen a transformation of the services they offer.

Today's agencies might be a "full service agency", which not only creates the classic advertising, but also does market research, provides content for digital platforms, stages events, engages in public relations and purchases all the media where the campaign will be shown. The aim is to offer a 360°-service to the client.

The way agencies get work is by pitching their idea to a prospective industry client who wishes to advertise. In this pitch, the agency presents its own credentials and an initial idea of what type of advertising they could create for the client and through which media it will be shown. If the client is happy with the presentation, a contract is signed and the real work begins.

Whether it is just the pitch or the full-on campaign that has been signed, the agency needs some important data from the client, which is usually put in a client briefing. Without this information, an advertising campaign might fail completely.

The client briefing

The client briefing is basically a set of instructions written by the client for the agency. According to Schneider and Pflaum (2000), the foundation of the briefing is the marketing strategy, which generally explains which products are offered to which target customers through which methods and in which market. The briefings are highly individual, but ideally should contain the following points:

1. Analysis of the status quo

- Information about competitors such as their market share and products of competitors
- Information on the market such as market data and data collected through experience
- Information about the product and the brand itself, including strengths and weaknesses, acceptance, origin or history
  External influences such as trends, politics or society
  The overall development of the marketing strategy

2. Objectives/strategy

Size of the campaign, type of campaign, plan of action.

3. The goal

Communication goals such as increasing usage of the product, penetration of the message into the market, change of consumer attitude or behaviour, change of the brand image, making the brand more known or more popular, etc. (Immediate goals to increase revenue and market share should not be the primary goal of an ad campaign because this is only possible through the implementation of the entire Marketing Mix.)

4. Target market

Customer profiling (socio-demographic structure, psychological typing). Demographics such as age, income, education etc. (this topic will be discussed in depth in Chapter 5).

5. Timing

When should this campaign be launched and how does it fit with other marketing activities?

6. Budget

How much is the brand ready to spend on the ad creation, the media and any additional service such as PR or events?

Agency briefing

Once the agency gets the job, it will turn the client's briefing into an internal briefing that will most likely change this into a so-called "agency briefing", which is used for internal purposes and actually getting the job done. It will be broken down into tasks for the different departments and employees, including the creative team (Schneider and Pflaum, 2000). The creative department and the creative director are the ones who are responsible for inventing the concept and the campaign. The creative concept is highly important to brands today as this can set them apart from competitors and convey a unique brand message to the consumer.

But whilst the creative process is highly important to a successful campaign, for the client it is rather "cheap" compared to how much it then costs to show the ad in various media channels. This is because the media channels can come with a hefty price.

An ad during the Super Bowl lasting only 30 seconds is world famous for costing several million dollars; *Vogue* magazine charges around $200,000 per one full colour page! The infamous September edition, often referred to as the "September Issue" consists of over 600 ad pages on average (of 900+ magazine pages in total) and you can calculate just how much the magazine makes in that one month. In 2013, the fashion magazine generated a total advertising revenue of 460 million US dollars (Statista). For fashion branding this means that only the most successful brands can afford to advertise there, squeezing out a lot of the competition. Start ups and small designers have to accept advertising in less glamorous media, or use public relations to get some editorial content in the top range magazines.

In brief, brands spend billions on advertising and media globally with a forecast of ad spending and ad volume of $552 billion and combined advertising, media and marketing spending surpassing $1 trillion in 2017 (GroupM, Aug. 2, 2016). Equally, the media channels and their advertising space is worth billions.

Considering the expenditure, the brand wants the ad to have the most impact, which is why it needs to be shown in the right media channels, at the right time and to the right audience.

This is where the media planning department starts working. This department, which can be part of the agency and in-house or a separate business has the task of finding and booking suitable media, using the client's budget. The goal is to reach the right audience at the right time with the right message to generate the desired response and then stay within the designated budget.

Media planners perform various calculations to find out how many individuals will be reached, how many times on average, how much this will cost when using the various media and how much impact this will have on the target audience.

Old and new communication channels

So what are today's media platforms where one can advertise?

Generally the advertising channels are separated into "BTL" and "ATL", which is short for Above the Line and Below the Line media. According to the Advertising Club (2011), these terms emerged in the 1950s and classify media into mass media and targeted media. Most of the available media channels have been in use for decades and are very effective (Manral, 2011).

ATL usually describes conventional media such as television and radio advertising, cinema advertising, print in magazines and newspapers, billboards as well as online ads (search engine ads). This type of communication targets a wider spread of audience, is not specific to individual consumers and has a very broad reach.

BTL advertising is more adjusted towards the individual (or smaller but specific target groups) using less conventional methods of advertising, such as sales promotions at the POS, public relations, direct marketing, fairs and trade shows, sponsoring, event marketing, product placement and most innovative communication forms such as guerilla marketing, ambient marketing, social media marketing, viral marketing and Bluetooth marketing. It can be a much cheaper, yet more effective way of reaching the consumer.

The choice of media channels will depend on several factors, such as the message which the brand wants to send out and the target customer group, the budget and the overall goal. It might choose to use ATL media, BTL media or mix and match from both.

Here are some examples of innovative ways to use brand communication.

Diesel, a brand that has an image of rebellious youth has used social media in a typically provocative yet innovative way by collaborating with popular adult dating apps. According to Adweek, the brand's creative director Nicola

ABOVE

Target:	Media:
Mass audience	Television advertising Radio advertising Cinema advertising Print in magazines and newspapers Billboards On-line ads (search engine ads etc.)

THE LINE

BELOW

Target:	Media:
Specific consumer group	Sales promotions at the POS Public relations Direct marketing Fairs and trade shows Sponsoring Event marketing Product placement Fashion film Innovative communication forms such as guerilla marketing, ambient marketing, social media marketing, viral marketing, Bluetooth marketing etc.

Figure 4.1 ATL (Above-the-Line) and BTL (Below-the-Line) media. Author's original illustration.

Formichetti stated that the online and offline worlds had completely merged, making digital "more real than reality" (Nudd, 2016). According to CEO Renzo Rosso, 80 per cent of Diesel's sales during a sales campaign can be attributed to consumers who have used the internet to check out the brand. Furthermore, in an interview with *Fashion Unfiltered*, Rosso stated that it is much easier for people today to find sex on the internet rather than to find a partner offline. "So it's not that we go to the porno channel with porno advertising, we just go there with sympathy and treat it like advertising in a magazine. We did it there because that's the way to live today" (Zarella, 2016).

Case example: MINI

The self-proclaimed lifestyle car brand MINI is known to have used guerrilla marketing to promote its car.

In 2009, the Amsterdam-based ad agency JWT produced a series of giant cardboard gift boxes which were placed on the streets of Amsterdam after Christmas, together with a heap of trash. Each box had a large diagram of the car with the words MINI COOPER and logo printed across the top, a barcode and price of 99, (currency not stated). It was made to look as if someone was gifted a Mini Cooper in this giant box and had discarded it and the wrapping. Images and videos of people passing the installation went viral shortly after.

In 2010, MINI once again surprised people with an installation on the beaches of Zandvoort (Holland) and in Knokke (Belgium) in 2011 with a campaign featuring a giant bottle, which seemingly had washed up on the shore with a life-size MINI car inside. The small bottles were found all over the Dutch/Belgian coastline.

For this campaign, MINI had teamed up with FEL, an Amsterdam-based agency specializing in brand experience. According to the agency

> Literally, FEL means FIERCE. And that's exactly what we do. Create fierce communication, with ideas and concepts that stand out. Using clever creativity, we're looking for more attention for the same budget. We want to create campaigns where consumers want to be part of. So our best campaigns are the ones where we there's no media budget involved, like this MINI case. For MINI we've been the BTL agency in Holland (activation, guerrilla marketing, social) for 5 years now, with occasional assignments in Belgium and for MINI international. We also work for brands like Sony, ABN, Save The Children, Neckermann and Shell.

Figure 4.2 A real MINI in a giant inflatable bottle on the beach of the Netherlands. Image kindly provided by creative agency FEL.

Table 4.1 Advertising costs as of 2016

Media type	Example of one purchased unit	Cost
TV: NBC	30-second commercial during the Super Bowl	$ 4.5 million[1]
TV: Fashion TV	Four weeks of 30-second commercials on air, five spots daily; global	€75000[2]
Billboard: London Underground	Two weeks on London Underground	£85,230[3]
	48 sheets – "Platinum", price per pack/per site	
Billboard in motion: Times Square NYC	1 year	$1.1 million and $4[4]
Radio: KKJZ LA	KKJZ, LA – one 15-second radio ad	$250[5]
Newspaper: *Daily Telegraph*	One full-colour page (not first page)	GBP 59,000[6]
Fashion print magazine: American *Vogue*	4th cover page in full colour	$ 245,709[7]
Supplement print magazine: *Financial Times* "How to Spend It"	Centre spread for one bi-monthly edition	$72,000[8]
Digital: Snapchat	"Discover Ad", daily rate	From $50,000 (note this is the price in 2016, which dropped significantly from $750,000 in 2014)[9]
Digital: Instagram	1000 impressions for a sponsored photo on Instagram (minimum order $200,000)	$35[10]
Digital: Instagram	Cost per click	20 cents to $2 per click (CPC) on an Instagram campaign.
		Cost per mille (CPM) focuses on impressions and costs around $5 per 1000 visitors on average.[11]

Notes for Table 4.1

1) www.bbc.com/news/world-us-canada-31064972
2) Fashion TV rate cards, September 2016.
3) Exterion Media, "London Underground, DLR & London Tramlink Rate Card 2016", www.exterionmedia.com/uk/new-to-outdoor/prices-and-rate-card
4) Adam Hayes, "The High Cost of Advertising in Times Square", *New York Times*, 23 Feb. 2015, www.investopedia.com/articles/investing/022315/high-cost-advertising-times-square.asp
5) KKJZ media data, October 2016.
6) *Daily Telegraph.*
7) American *Vogue.*
8) *Financial Times.*
9) Wallaroomedia, 2016, http://wallaroomedia.com/snapchat-advertising-cost
10) Ad Age, http://adage.com/article/news/costs-ad-prices-tv-mobile-billboards/297928 www.bbc.com/news/magazine-30113027
11) Influence Marketing Hub, https://influencermarketinghub.com/how-much-does-it-cost-to-advertise-on-instagram

According to Jay Conrad Levinson, Guerrilla marketing "works because it's simple to understand, easy to implement and outrageously inexpensive". He should know, as he was the one who invented the term back in the 1980s (Levinson, 2016).

So how expensive is "outrageously inexpensive" and what sort of costs are we comparing it to you might wonder. Let's see which of the ATL and BTL are most expensive and which ones are cheap.

Most media will publish their advertising cost on line. It can be tricky to find it via the website, but if you Google the media's name and the word "rate card" or "media kit" (sometimes "media pack" or "media data") you will be able to access the data.

Table 4.1 shows some examples of what advertising can cost, as of 2016, in various fashionable cities, upscale printed media, niche radio and digital platforms – from very reasonable to excruciatingly high.

Consumer trust

According to research conducted by Statista in 2016, every second person stated that they trusted TV ads and e-mails they signed up for whilst other types of online ads scored much lower, with only one in every three consumers trusting online video or display ads. (However, this statistic would leave 50 per cent of the audience which mistrusts advertising.)

Consumer trust in advertising mirrors to a certain extent the amount of money invested in different ad mediums and TV is still the biggest advertising medium globally. The United States, as the country of origin for modern advertising practice, is still the biggest advertising market in the world.

Interview with Thorsten Voigt

Thorsten Voigt has been a copywriter and creative director at Serviceplan for more than nine years, and recently switched to freelancing.

Figure 4.3 Thorsten Voigt.

Q: Do brands choose to work with just one agency now that advertising agencies are offering a 360° service?

TV: Large, successful brands like Adidas, Nike, BMW like to choose the best possible agencies for each communication strategy. So they will take the leading agency for their print advertising, another leading agency for their PR and yet another for digital strategies. In-house the brand usually has a vision and smart marketing plan, which ensures that all their agencies create concepts that fit their vision. However, smaller brands might choose the one-stop option and use just one agency for all of their communication needs.

Q: How do brands find their agency?

TV: Through recommendations or by directly contacting the best possible agencies, if that is what they are looking for. Serviceplan for example, has a really good reputation in Germany and a top creative ranking.

Q: What happens then?

TV: A client will ask five or six agencies to do a pitch for him. Oftentimes the brands will not pay for the pitch (or a small pitch fee) which might cost the agency tens of thousands of Euros to prepare. This is because the agency develops the strategy, creates nearly finished layouts and mood-movies to sell the idea.

Q: When the client has chosen you over the others, what are the next steps?

TV: The consultant gets a briefing from the client and develops a strategy on how to reach the target customer. This strategy information and the goal of the campaign is passed on to the creative team who has to develop the campaign.

Q: What does the creative team do and who is involved in creating the campaign?

TV: For a campaign, the team consists of a senior copywriter and a senior art director. The creative director makes sure that their work is creative enough and fits the briefing and strategy. The strategy comes from the consultants who received all the relevant information from the client. Other people who might be involved are online experts if you are creating a 360° strategy, media planners and others. The creative process itself is quite tenacious because the first idea we get is usually not the best one. The first idea is the one that will come to the minds of many. We look for the one that has not been done before and is unique. Many ideas get tossed in the garbage and you might work extra hours while brainstorming.

Q: How do you know which ideas have not been done before?

TV: In the creative department, you have to keep up to date and know what the competition is doing. In a way, everything has already been done at some point, but it's the fresh take that counts and we try to use new impressions and new combinations to create something great.

Q: What skills do you need to work on the creative team?

TV: As an art director you need to know all the graphic programs and understand layouts, illustrators need to be good with drawing, and a copywriter just needs to be really good with language and just know words. The trick is to make a point in as few words as possible.

Q: How about media planning?

V: It can be an in-house department or a separate firm that the agency closely works with. The agency might recommend the media firm, but ultimately it's the client's choice which one he uses. He might just want a creative campaign.

Q: What happens if you receive a request from two competing brands, let's say Nike and Adidas, who want a campaign from your agency?

TV: Some clients will request that you do not work with a competitor they want to be the only client of a certain segment. Others request a different creative team to work on their account if they know that you work on a close competitor. It really depends on the brands.

Q: How are fashion brands different from other clients?

TV: Fashion brands can easily do it all the creative work themselves and might not need an agency for that. They know photography, model casting, fittings, etc. They might need help with the media planning.

Q: What about the classic advertising channels, the so-called ATL? Are they dying out?

TV: It's still very important. But ultimately the communication channel depends on the target customer. A young person is always in touch with their mobile device, while an older person will read a magazine or newspaper. Billboards and posters will probably remain effective for everyone because when we are out and about we look at the street ads.

Creative direction at the agency and the fashion brand

Large fashion companies and especially those of the luxury segment usually have one famous creative director or sometimes a creative duo of directors, like Maria Grazia Chiuri and Pierpaolo Piccioli at Valentino until 2016. There is no need to rely on an agency for the creative input because the creative director has a certain vision for the brand's advertising, photography and promotion and oftentimes is gifted in all these areas.

Thus the creative director might be engaged in a broad spectrum of creating the fashion imagery used to promote the brand. In the case of Karl Lagerfeld, he was – like many creative directors – a multi-talent and designed buildings, interiors, published books, engaged in photography and other very creative practices.

For the brand Chanel, he was known to cast models, take photos and even shoot advertorial movies himself. When he had a new muse, he or she would appear on the catwalk and in the promotional images, just like Claudia Schiffer, Tilda Swinton, Cara Delevingne, Brad Kroenig, Baptiste Giabiconi or more recently Kendall Jenner.

In 2015, *The Observer* reported that Kendall Jenner was styled by infamous Grace Coddington and then photographed by Karl Lagerfeld in person for a spread in *Vogue*'s September issue. She also got to play with Karl Lagerfeld's famous cat Choupette.

For Marc Jacobs, his muse has been Sofia Coppola who starred in several ad campaigns for him over the span of 13 years, including for the perfumes Blush and Daisy.

If the creative director is not taking the photos him or herself, or has a talented movie director to help, the fashion house will closely work with a fashion photographer to produce high quality images and communicate the brand's vision.

At fashion brands, especially luxury brands, the advertising and visuals for promotion are often created in house, with the creative director giving the vision for the brand's overall look. He or she might be involved in the casting of models, styling and photography of the campaigns, aligning it with the overall message of the brand.

Brands, which have distinct creative vision and heritage, thrive on a creative director. He or she has the task of delivering a unique creative vision which will influence all brand elements, from the collections to the brand communication, forming a unique brand identity. This is the USP of the fashion brand and therefore a creative director's vision might better feel what type of visual communication is suitable.

The great influence on the fashion brand has been documented in the popular and somewhat voyeuristic fashion documentaries, starting with Loic Prigent in 2005, who filmed Karl Lagerfeld at Chanel by following him around. Since then many more of such documentaries have emerged, showing Yves Saint-Laurent and his partner, Marc Jacobs at Louis Vuitton, Raf Simmons at Dior, Frida Giannini at Gucci, Valentino in his many homes and other creative directors hard at work. The documentaries show a secret world behind closed doors of the most celebrated luxury brands and their temporary geniuses, leaving either due to old age, being ushered out by the brand or getting poached by others. In the last few years the luxury fashion business has evolved into the Mad Hatter's tea party where all of a sudden everyone changes places but remains at the same table. These increasingly frequent movements have been named the game of "Fashion Musical Chairs" by editors from *Vanity Fair*, *The New York Times*, *Vogue* and *Harpers Bazaar*.

When the creative director dies or departs, the luxury fashion brands face the challenge and the opportunity of revitalizing the brand identity with a new creative.

For instance, in the case of Yves Saint-Laurent, the brand saw a 180° make-over when Hedi Slimane took the creative reins in 1999. He moved the headquarters of the brand from Paris to Los Angeles, changed the look from romantic and feminine to grunge and unisex and brought in sneakers, sickeningly thin models in his much criticized ad campaigns and a monochrome colour palate. He is famously known for having created most of the fashion ad campaigns where he cast the models, styled and photographed them himself.

But what made many fashion veterans scream was the change of the brand's name from Yves Saint-Laurent (YSL) to Saint Laurent. There was a small revolt of printed T-Shirts which read "Ain't Laurant without Yves" in a clever word play.

Despite all the commotion, his new vision for the brand was a commercial success and brought the aging brand high profits within a short time.

In 2016 Slimane left the company, and a new creative director is in place: Anthony Vaccarello who has to live up to the fame and success of his predecessor.

Similar influences on a brand's identity and its communication can be observed with the brands Dior, Balmain, Gucci, Lanvin, Burberry, Balenciaga, Givenchy and others.

The challenges for fashion media today

Although advertising today uses all sorts of media channels, including online advertising and social media, most fashion brands (especially in the luxury segment) still use the traditional fashion magazine as the main platform for advertising and surprisingly it still works for them. There is a long history of advertising in fashion magazines dating back to the first issues of *Harper's Bazaar* or *Vogue*. Miller (2013) traces fashion magazines back to eighteenth-century France.

As the cover and fold-out pages are highly expensive, there is often a lot of competition between luxury brands who want to secure the best possible spot. Furthermore, if brands spend a certain amount of money on advertising in the magazine, the chances are very high that the brand will also appear in an editorial of the issue.

When you look at the rate card or media kit of a glossy magazine, there will also be prices for digital media such as tablets and smartphones as well as demographic data on the core reader of the publication.

The digital channels are becoming increasingly important whilst print notes a steady decline.

Business of Fashion wrote in August 2016 that most editorial content is currently consumed digitally, which publishing houses not only acknowledge but also embed in their future strategy.

"Indeed, Hearst, Condé Nast and Time Inc. have each announced plans to significantly boost their digital offerings [which] means trimming the budgets of their print magazines" (Hoang, 2016).

In a snapshot of the readership platforms of *Harper's Bazaar* in March 2015, you can see that of 5,909,000 readers, 257,1000 – or more than a third – are looking at digital content either on the internet or on a mobile device. In addition to the regular print, there are digital editions and as a statistic both are put together rather than looking at them separately.

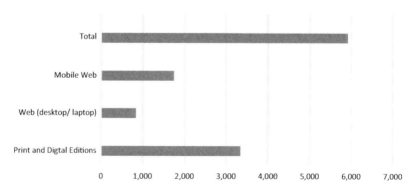

Figure 4.4 The statistic presents information on the number of *Harper's Bazaar* readers in the United States in March 2015, by platform. The magazine reached 1.74 million readers over the mobile web. Author's own illustration, based on Statista, 2016.

The fashion magazine is still a classic choice for fashion advertising despite of e-commerce and m-commerce. However, as digital media becomes increasingly popular with consumers, fashion brands and fashion publications need to catch up urgently.

So what is the future for fashion print magazine? And how does this affect the traditional print advertising?

Let's look at the average revenue of magazines from advertising: According to Statista, from 2010 to 2015, *Vogue* magazine has been making USD 42 million on average every year in advertising revenue. During the same period, *Elle* magazine made USD 38 million on average every year (PZ-online, 2016).

One short-term reflex type of strategy by fashion "glossies" is to increase the price for their magazines. This is because apart from the advertising revenue, the magazines live off the circulation or amount of copies sold. However, this cannot be done blindly. The publications need to analyse the current target readers and evaluate which type of platform corresponds to which age group. Generally it seems that generation Z and Y are predominantly consuming their fashion editorials on mobile devices. This is where fashion ads should be happening, too. But the division by age and generation closes when it comes to luxury fashion, which was revealed in a recent study by McKinsey and Altagamma in 2015. Older luxury consumers also like to use the same digital and mobile platforms (Remy, Catena, Durand-Servoingt, 2015) or switching to advertising for digital platforms might thus be lucrative as it reaches many age groups and many potential readers.

Looking at platforms such as Instagram, Snapchat, WeChat and YouTube etc. and other globally used apps there is room to place editorials and advertising which can link back to an extensive version in the printed edition thus closing the publishing and ad loop.

The interesting and challenging element is that the popularity of the digital platforms fluctuates strongly and changes rapidly – something that sturdy fashion magazines might not (yet) be used to, because they have a mostly unchanging history of decades. With digital platforms, they can go in and out of style within a few years or a few months, their popularity can differ from country to country, and they are popular with varying age groups. The new challenge for the classic fashion magazines is to keep up with the changing nature of digital content and their audiences and in order to do so, they must invest in new talent – the digital natives who grew up with those platforms. Until recently, some of the sales teams of those platforms might be older and not digital natives themselves so it is crucial for their success to employ young people as part of their team and "train" the older generations.

If the brand does not want to employ digital natives, it can work together with a media agency which helps brands to clearly define the right channels in order to reach the target customer. This type of agency will make sure that the advertising message reaches its maximum potential. It is solely focused on getting the brand's message and content to the target audience by using the most suitable media channel. Furthermore, the agency can negotiate prices and book slots or space with the channel providers and platforms directly.

The interview below shows some insights about the work such an agency does.

Interview with a renowned media agency in Germany

Q: How large is your agency?

A: We have a very large international network of agencies, which has about 80,000 employees.

Q: How would you sum up the services that you offer to your clients?

A: We offer our clients comprehensive support in terms of all media activities. To put it short, we make sure that our clients' products (or services) and their advertising campaigns reach the potential customers at the right place and at the right time. We work out the suitable target group by analysing and defining it, we analyse and interpret the entire market and the specific competitors of our clients. We develop strategies for exactly how and where the products or services should be marketed, continuously lead the entire campaign management on behalf of our client and optimize the return on investment and much more. We are always at the side of our clients and continuously consult them on anything and everything media.

Q: How many clients do you work with?

A: Overall, our agency deals with more than 150 different clients.

Q: Do you have clients from the fashion industry and are there any differences when working with them?

A: Yes, we have fashion and accessories luxury brands as well as online retailers. When working with fashion clients, one has to be open to new trends and be quick to "jump on the band wagon" when a new trend emerges in order to stay ahead in a very competitive market. Furthermore, social media is a very important topic (especially Facebook or Instagram) as it appeals to the target market and is convenient for them.

Q: Do you work with advertising agencies or directly with the marketing and communication departments of the various companies?

A: We work directly with the marketing and communications departments of companies and brands, with constant exchange of ideas and joint planning.

As a media agency, we then take care of the realization of the media strategy and manage the campaign. Sometimes we connect with other agencies – but those are PR agencies or creative agencies. Since we are responsible for the media performance of a product our work may cross over into PR activities and this is why we are also in constant exchange with the PR agency. The same goes for creative agencies, because we have to know the creative work in order to assess which channels might work best.

Q: Have media preferences changed over the last years?

A: Yes, and very much so! TV is still a popular type of media, which has a high reach for a commercial. However, today there is a lot of streaming mainly because people work more, are out and about and have very little time for classic TV. This means there is a strong trend in increasingly using online videos or video-on-demand because it gives more flexibility and choice as to when you want to watch your favourite show. In addition, it is more pleasant for consumers because commercials are much shorter during streaming than on classic TV.

Moreover, global digitization plays an increasingly important role. Everyone is everywhere, always online, constantly leaving data behind and simultaneously being tracked. Which means that many brands and products now have to play off their precisely target-oriented and "catchy" advertising messages against each other in a highly competitive market of the digital worlds.

Even though there are many possibilities to place an advertising message, this has to happen in the right environment and with the right message, or else it will not motivate anyone to buy or consume but rather be perceived as "annoying" and "disruptive", and enhance a negative connotation in the consumers' minds.

Considering digitalization, one should not underestimate the power of social media and its current role. This is precisely the virtual place where many consumers are at during their leisure time. And during leisure time they are relaxed and more open to advertising messages of all kinds. This is where they can be reached extremely well with a suitable offer or even product information. Here it is easier to like a page, to be redirected to another website or to interact with a product in a different way.

Especially in this regard, the so-called Programmatic Advertising is gaining increasing importance where purchase and sale of advertising space happens in real time. This offers specific possibilities of targeting (the brand buys media directly) and reaching the perfectly suitable consumer by analysing his online surfing behaviour in advance. The consumer is in the right environment, at the right time and receives the right ad message.

Ethical considerations

What sort of ethics must an advertising agency or media agency consider?

If you look back at the history of targeted advertising and marketing, any client and any product was accepted and the main goal was to launch a successful campaign. This was true for selling cigarettes to women (including pregnant women as demonstrated by ads of the mid-twentieth century), alcohol and unhealthy food, slimming products, overpriced fashion and cosmetics and products which would not meet standards pertaining to social, environmental and sometimes even legal codes of good practice. The ethical marketer must carefully examine the product and the company and decide whether it is something worth promoting as this promotion naturally reaches hundreds, thousands or sometimes millions of people. A choice will affect the public and this choice must be made responsibly.

There are several advertising agencies that have made a strong stance on their ethical practice. For example, Plant is a self-proclaimed ethical and socially conscious agency based in London, England, which focuses on social change, charity, NGO and sustainable businesses and products. Their credo is to make the best decisions every day which concern the ethical impact they make.

Furthermore, the Institute for Advertising Ethics (IAE) aims to "inspire advertising, public relations and marketing communications professionals to practice the highest personal ethics in the creation and distribution of commercial information to consumers".

The IAE is built on eight principles and practices which convey what all forms of communication should be based on, including advertising, public relations, marketing communications, news and editorial.

The principles include truth and ethical standards in their daily work, abiding by the law, clearly marking sponsored content by bloggers (vs. a blogger's own opinion), and special precautions when addressing vulnerable members of society such as children among others. The eight principle is arguably the most important one for any marketing professional: "(...) members of the team creating ads should be given permission to express internally their ethical concerns" (Snyder, 2011).

Discussing ethical concerns is the first step to creating awareness within a marketing company and the logical second step is then to integrate the best practice into the projects.

Further reading

Bartlett, D. (2013) *Fashion Media: Past and Present.* London: Bloomsbury Academic.

Diamond, J. (2015) *Retail Advertising and Promotion.* New York: Fairchild.

Fennis, B. M. and Stroebe, W. (2010) *The Psychology of Advertising.* Abingdon, UK: Psychology Press.

Keaney, M. (2007) *Fashion & Advertising. (World's Top Photographers Workshops).* Mies: RotoVision.

Kelley, L. D., Jugenheimer, D. W. and Sheehan, K. (2015) *Advertising Media Planning: A Brand Management Approach.* 4th edn. New York: Routledge.

Lane, W. R., Whitehill Kink, K. and Russel, T. J. (2008) *Kleppner's Advertising Procedure.* 17th edn. New Jersey: Pearson Prentice Hall.

Lea-Greenwood, G. (2012) *Fashion Marketing Communications.* John Wiley & Sons.

Moore, G. (2012) *Basics Fashion Management: Fashion Promotion 02: Building a Brand Through Marketing and Communication.* London: Bloomsbury Publishing.

Matharu, S. (2011) *Advertising Fashion Brands to the UK Ethnic Market: How Ethnic Models Influence Ethnic Consumer Purchase Behaviour.* Verlag, Germany: VDM.

Snyder, W. S. (2001) Principles and Practices for Advertising Ethics. Institute for Advertising Ethics. Available at: www.aaf.org/_PDF/AAF%20Website%20Content/513_Ethics/IAE_Principles_Practices.pdf

Tungate, M. (2007) *Adland: A Global History of Advertising.* London: Kogan Page.

Advertising news, sites and resources:

Advertising Age. https://adage.com

Ad Asia Online. www.adasiaonline.com

Adweek. www.adweek.vom

Branding in Asia. https://brandinginasia.com

Campaign Asia. www.campaignasia.com

Campaign. www.camaignlive.co.uk

Digiday. https://digiday.com

The Drum. www.thedrum.com

MediaPost. www.mediapost.com

Social media, blogs and opinion-leaders $\quad$ **5**

Who is leading your opinion?

Chapter topics

The general meaning of an opinion leader

Two-step flow of communication

The precursor to the "Two-Step Flow of Communication" hypothesis which emerged in 1944 was the brain-child of Paul Lazarsfeld, Bernard Berelson and Hazel Gaudet. The purpose of the study was to examine what influenced people to vote during political campaigns. The research showed unexpected results as the biggest influence for the people were personal and quite informal contacts rather than exposure to radio or newspaper. Based on these findings, it was Katz and Lazarsfeld who developed the two-step flow theory of mass communication that is still widely used today or has been amended and developed further for present times.

As the name states, the theory is based solely on two steps of information flow: At first, information from the mass media will reach opinion leaders, who are people paying attention to and following the mass media. The opinion leaders will interpret this information and being quite influential, they will disseminate their interpretation to a large group of people with whom they are socially connected.

(University of Twente, 2017)

This model, which was first developed in the 1940s (again the golden age of marketing innovation in the USA as mentioned in the previous chapters), is relevant yet again in the twenty-first century when blogging emerged. It is possible to achieve a certain reaction of a mass of people by first influencing the opinion leader accordingly, pre-calculating how he or she will re-distribute the information.

Blogging essentially works the same way: There is one blogger who has followers. This blogger will receive sponsored goods and information from brands which are then presented in a personal, authentic style on the blogger's media channel. The information reaches the blogger's followers and his or her opinion leads the opinion of a multitude of followers.

The only change today is an evolvement of cross communication between the followers, strengthening the message which is spread.

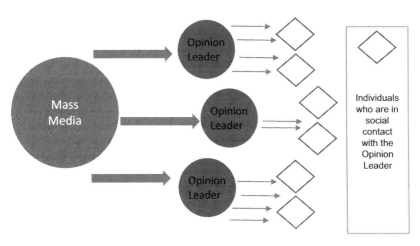

Figure 5.1 Two-step communication model. Author's own interpretation of original by Lazarsfeld.

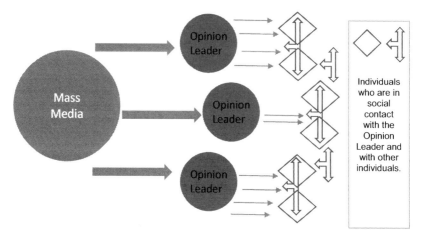

Figure 5.2 Two-step communication model applied for use today. Author's own interpretation based on original by Lazarsfeld.

> The Two-Step-Flow model by Lazarsfeld in the 1940s can still be used today to demonstrate how opinion leaders bring a message to their followers, thus spreading it to very specific groups.
>
> For a brand it can be beneficial not to broadly spread a message to everyone possible, but to seek out an opinion leader who will get the message to those who will certainly respond to it positively.

Understanding blogging and what it can do for fashion brands

In 2016/17 blogging was already more than 10 years old and had its own history. It began as a sort of personal diary, a diary that is not quite yours nor that secret because its aim was for everyone to read it and comment on it. To the reader, it offered 24 hours a day access and was location independent at the same time.

In the first years of the new millennium, people began setting up personal style blogs and showcasing fashion on them. One of the very first people to do so was the now famous Scott Schuman with his "The Sartorialist" blog. Schuman (2005) states in his biography that he "began The Sartorialist with the idea of creating a two-way dialogue about the world of fashion and its relationship to daily life". He posted street shots of stylish people sharing his creative life as well as perspective on fashion with the world.

Schuman would be considered an "Industry Blogger" which means that he is an expert with a background in the industry, either fashion journalism, design, styling or similar. In this particular case, he had a degree in apparel merchandizing and photography.

The other type of blogger is often called the "Citizen Blogger". According to Gwyneth Moore (2012) this person is a "passionate consumer of fashion", sharing their lifestyle and clothing habits, style and opinions with followers.

In 2016, about 10 years after the first blogs emerged, there were hundreds of thousands of successful and high-earning bloggers and it has become a staple of our digital landscape.

Mark Briggs writes that bloggers, unlike journalists, have the privilege of far more freedom in what they write, who they talk to and what other people they link their posts to. They might start out small but as more people read their blog they will reach a tipping point after which the audience takes over. This is a benchmark that indicates when a blog has become really successful (and profitable) (Briggs, 2016).

The power of blogs is so evident, that even the classic printed media have resorted to launching their own blogs on their websites, like *Vogue Magazine* who poached Suzy Menkes away from a career at *The International Herald Tribune* (spanning 25 years) to become the editor of *Vogue*'s own blog in 2014.

Equally, about 18 per cent of private bloggers turn to the help of professional editors before posting and around 50 per cent ask someone to look over the post before making it live, as a 2016 survey of Orbitmedia revealed (Crestodina, 2018).

Blogging has become a lucrative business sector, and often requires an office with staff who run the blog. It is rare that one witnesses the emergence of a completely new profession within their lifetime, particularly within the fashion industry.

So how exactly is a blogger interesting to a fashion brand? Here is a best-case list of characteristics and business options a fashion brand might be looking for when it wants to do business with a blogger:

- The fashion blogger X is in tune with the current trends and his posts are highly relevant to his or her audience.
- X comes across as authentic and is considered an authority in fashion.
- The content of the posts is highly visual (photo/video), which is very important in fashion; it is original and creative.
- The content is informative so that the brand's message can get transferred. X has a good writing style and is an excellent communicator (including grammar and spelling) when it comes to storytelling.
- X is happy to be sent to report directly on fashion events, sometimes live.
- The blog posts by X can be timed with other important marketing activities of the brand such as store-opening, shows, product launches etc.

- X has several thousand or hundred thousand followers and they are a perfect fit for the brand.
- The followers are the correct target group for the fashion brand in terms of age, gender, income, fashion preference, shopping habits etc.
- The followers react to the blogger's content so a high rate of engagement can be expected.
- X does not promote competing brands or X does promote competing brands, but there is minimal risk of losing customers this way.
- The blogger is active on different platforms such as blog, YouTube, Instagram, Twitter etc. The brand can choose to do a campaign either on several platforms or just the strongest one.

What brands get in return for working with a blogger:

- Engagement
- Reach
- Numbers immediately measurable
- Targeting the right consumers who are likely to respond positively to the message
- Potential increase in product or service purchases

If a brand and a blogger are the right fit, the amount a blogger earns can be substantial. In 2011, *The Sartorialist* stated in a controversial interview with The Talks that American Apparel bought advertising space on his site for one year and Net-a-Porter for the rest of 2010:

> So those two ads alone are a good fraction of a million dollars: more than a quarter million and less than a half a million. [...] My audience is so much larger than everybody else's that advertisers, well at least American Apparel told me that I am not in their internet budget. My order is so big and they have to pay so much that I am actually in their magazine budget. That comes from having a good size audience.

Interestingly this statement caused quite a stir in the fashion world, being quoted numerous times on other blogs and websites. However, the original publishers of the interview no longer have it on their website (Oystermag, 2011).

Research is still emerging on how social media really works or why indeed it does. But some say that searching, finding, liking, sharing, commenting and the self-presentation on social media is deeply embedded in our primal instincts and connects to feelings of reward. "Dopamine is stimulated by unpredictability, by small bits of information, and by reward cues—pretty much the exact conditions of social media. The pull of dopamine is so strong that studies have shown tweeting is harder for people to resist than cigarettes and alcohol" https://blog.bufferapp.com/psychology-of-social-media

It is highly likely that more psychological and behavioural research will be conducted in the years to come on the phenomena of social media, including harmful or unethical effects.

Interview with blogger Navaz Batliwalla aka Disneyrollergirl

Figure 5.3 Navaz Batliwalla aka Disneyrollergirl. With kind permission of Navaz Batliwalla and Emma Miranda Moore.

Q: I believe that you have had professional training and a fashion industry background. Could you please tell me a bit more about that?

NB: My background isn't design but fashion media. I have worked in print and digital publishing for over 20 years including working as the fashion director of *CosmoGIRL!* and the launch fashion editor of *Grazia India*. In 1999 while I was a freelance stylist, I was approached to contribute a fashion advice column and articles to a women's online publication (called Handbag.com which was owned by Telegraph media and later Hearst). I also contributed to their discussion forums, which I enjoyed very much as I felt this gave me a great insight into the consumer. For me, the forums were almost a precursor to social media.

Q: Do you think it is essential to have this background to be a successful fashion influencer or would you say that those with no formal training do it just as well?

NB: The profession of 'fashion influencer' is so broad and new it is difficult to answer this question. If you are writing an informed blog and want access to certain brands' workshops, design studios or business decision makers then it helps to have a certain credibility and level of professionalism. For luxury brands, the world of digital influencers is still rather unknown so they prefer to stick to what they know, i.e. print journalists or those who have proven credentials. For me, having those established relationships meant I already had 'access' and a level of trust.

On the other hand, if you're someone posting outfit pictures on Instagram in which the subject is you rather than brands then it's not necessary to have a fashion industry background. That said, any experience of business is a benefit and the fashion industry has many unspoken codes. Of course influencers have agents and managers now, but to understand business, legalities, negotiating and just the ins and outs of the industry is a huge advantage.

Q: How many years have you been a fashion influencer and is this your full-time job and career now?

NB: I have been blogging at Disneyrollergirl.net for nine years. I combine it with freelance writing and consulting which means that although the blogging generates income, I'm not beholden to it and don't need to monetize every single opportunity. Being more choosy increases my credibility and value.

Q: How much time do you need to spend weekly to tend to your social media activities?

NB: Sadly I'm a one-man band so for me social media is 24/7. However, as a fashion writer it is also my news source.

Q: After so many years, which channel works best for you and why?

NB: Twitter is my best channel for information and follower numbers, but Instagram is better for direct engagement with readers.

Q: Do you use a tool or platform to manage all your social media accounts? (Crowdbooster, Socia Flow, Tweepi etc.)

NB: No, I do everything manually.

Q: How important is it to be based in a large fashion capital, like London?

NB: For the work I do it's essential. It gives me creative stimulation and also allows me to create visually interesting content. Networking and maintaining relationships with publicists is an important part of what I do and that has to be done in London.

Q: What is your USP or how are you unique and different from other bloggers?

NB: I am an established 'fashion insider' and have been working in the industry for a long time. I write from an informed journalistic perspective so the blog is not about me but my observations on fashion, the industry, retail and anything in those spheres that's emerging. So subjects such as the rise of nail art, men's grooming, the emerging markets, entry level fine jewellery, gender-neutral fashion, social media, content and commerce, luxury craft, 3D printing, cosplay and omni channel retail have been covered by me early on. Once they start to infiltrate the mainstream, I move on to explore other emerging areas.

Q: Do you ever turn off your phone, computer, ignore all messages and go out for a walk?

NB: Of course.

Q: How did fashion brands start approaching you back in the day?

NB: For the first three years I didn't have an email address for my blog. Eventually I decided to get one so I didn't miss out on commercial opportunities. I was anonymous at the time but decided to 'go public'. Brands would email me and invite me to press days, fashion shows or coffee meetings to understand how I work. But I also knew many brands already so they felt safe with me as a blogger.

Q: If possible please name some brands you have worked for.

NB: Chloe, Dior, Levi's, Club Monaco, Chanel, Smythson.

Q: What would you say the brands are looking for in a blogger/influencer with whom they'd like to work? And what do you, as an influencer, expect from them?

NB: The best and most clued up brands expect a genuine interest in their brand/sector/product and a real point of view. The not-so-good brands expect lots of clicks and sales and do not always have realistic expectations (i.e. they don't research the blog to check it's a good fit). I have high expectations and prefer to work with brands on projects over a long period of time rather than one off campaigns. That way I invest time to understand the brand and create lasting content that works for both of us. I have to consider all of my channels including social media and Pinterest to make sure the content has the best reach. Often the brand only cares about your unique users which is short sighted.

Q: Is it usually the marketing team or the PR team or the advertising team that works with you?

NB: It's a combination of sales and PR. They usually go via my agent in the first instance.

Q: Do the brands have a clear vision of what they want to communicate and how you can do that?

NB: Increasingly yes.

Q: How much freedom do brands grant you, also in terms of creativity and the channels you use?

NB: It varies. The most high-end brands give me the most freedom, they take time to nurture a lasting relationship and make sure the brand and product is a good fit. Quite often I will go to them with an idea. The more mainstream brands tend to be box tickers. 'We need this many eyeballs, we have this much budget, let's get ten bloggers to do the same campaign, here's the hashtag'. It's a blanket approach and not very interesting. It's easier for them to manage this way than managing ten very different individual campaigns, even if a tailored approached would probably be more engaging to each person's audience.

Q: Blogging (influencer work) has turned into a whole new profession and some of the successful bloggers need to employ entire teams, including photographers, digital artists, etc. Do you employ any "helpers" or can you do it all by yourself?

NB: It's not sustainable or scalable to do it yourself if it's a full time job. If I'm doing a collaboration, I need to work with photographers and models. I have a tech person to help with the back end from time to time, but in an ideal world would have the means to pay for ongoing tech services. Obviously I want to be informed but keeping up with developments in Web design, social media, affiliates and so on is too much for one person after a certain point. I do have an agent to help with negotiations and some production work but they don't always have the manpower to go out looking for new clients. So I have to do a certain amount of personal brand building and relationship building myself which is time consuming. The ideal scenario at my stage is to have an assistant who I can train up so that they can help out with all the elements from creative to business.

Q: There is a stereotypical idea of what a blogger's life is like, based on the imagery that they communicate: Sleeping in and waking up in 5-star hotels, eating fancy food, being chauffeured around to fashion events and clinking glasses with all the "it" people. All this while wearing designer clothes and getting lots of dosh for it. Please give us a wake-up call and insight on the reality!

NB: The reality is of course nothing like this. People need to understand that like all creative industries, the above scenario may be the reality for the 0.01 per cent, but as with other fashion jobs, we all collude in portraying an illusion. Why? Because the illusion and fantasy of fashion is what pays our bills. The reality is more like spending around four hours on each blog post (researching, writing, editing, coding, taking/editing/resizing/tagging images), promoting with social media, engaging with followers/commenters, answering up to 250 emails a day, managing PR's expectations on whether you can attend an event/meeting or write about an unsolicited product you've been sent, attend press days, shop openings etc. to 'support the brand', keeping up with every new platform that comes along, making sure your outfit is on brand every time you go to an event, in case you are photographed or filmed. Quite often I work until am as I am more productive when there are no emails coming in. Yet I'm still expected to attend breakfast meetings at 9am. A lot of it is just like any other desk job. But of course we don't talk about that! Creating outfit posts or editorial shoots really does take some considerable pre production, post production and endless social media promotion. There's a lot of donkey work connected to it.

Q: Would you say that blogging or being a social media influencer is more advertising or is it public relations? Perhaps it is journalism based on advertorials?

NB: At the level where it's being monetized it's a combination of all four. It should be a balance and I think when the advertising and commercial aspects overshadow everything else, then you have a problem. The readers get bored and your content has no substance.

Q: Are there any bloggers who inspired you when you were starting out and who do you look up to now?

NB: Most of the bloggers I looked up to in the early days aren't around any more. I don't know if I looked up to them as much as admiring their writing and tone of voice. I admired The Sartorialist for his photography. Now, I admire him for keeping his integrity, and also Garance Doré for maintaining a unique tone of voice and visual identity. I wouldn't say I 'look up' to them though.

Q: What comes when all the blogging has been done? There are bloggers turning into designers, others (like you!) publish serious books. Blogs based on personal youth and beauty can't be eternal. What do you see in this profession for the next 10 to 20 years?

NB: No one said blogging was or should be about personal youth and beauty although commercially it feels like it has become that. I think it has become saturated with the new wave who came along because they want the fame and ego-stroking rather than because they have something to say. This wave will subside once they realize there are no long-term gains to be had. I feel as a profession, blogging will soon have to be regulated and may then lose its charm. So, at some point, as an industry, there will be a merging of blogs and traditional online media. The blogs with integrity will not be commercialized but will continue as hobby blogs.

Q: What inspires you to keep going? What do you envision for your influencer future?

NB: I don't envision my influencer future as such. My goal is to maintain a living as a freelance fashion editor and creative consultant whether that's in print or online or in advertising/marketing, but to maintain an outlet for my personal point of view. That could be writing, moving image (in the near future), or even virtual reality broadcasting. I am much happier creating content behind the scenes;

the medium is not important. What keeps me going in that respect is a deep love of fashion, the industry, creativity and observing and analyzing the changes. But I very much value having the insider access, so my ambition is to maintain that.

Celebrity endorsements and what they can do for a fashion brand

As was noted in Chapter 2, the idea of a celebrity opinion leader is nothing new. Queen Elizabeth I, Napoleon and Queen Victoria – just to name a few – were political leaders who strategically shaped and influenced the opinion of their people (followers) and fashion. In fact, being affiliated with a royal "celebrity" was a fantastic promotional tool for merchants and artisans of that era. Cope and Maloney (2016) believe that the Royal Warrant, which was first introduced in the UK in the twelfth century, was one way to help highly skilled artisans to grow their business. This included tailors, cobblers and dressmakers who might have had the warrant until this day.

In nineteenth-century France, Empress Eugenie was an avid fashion leader and endorsed her couturier Charles Frederick Worth who is said to have been the first designer to put a name (and a brand) on his lavish creations. Associating with royals, even today, is something designers and brands strive for. For instance, Elizabeth Emanuel and her husband were catapulted into stardom after they designed Princess Diana's wedding dress. Some decades later, Kate, the Duchess of Cambridge, became an opinion-leader and fashion celebrity herself, promoting British designers by wearing their creations. By choosing to mostly wear UK high-street brands, those dresses were instantly sold out in stores and online, so much so that this was dubbed "the Kate effect".

Now let's see who else apart from royals could be considered a celebrity in the twenty-first century. Is it a famous actor or athlete? A singer? Is it a reality TV star, scientist or activist? Perhaps it is an iconic designer, another brand or a model. For the needs of today's fashion, it can be any of those and many more but there has to be a common denominator.

In this context, celebrities have three things in common which are attractive to brands: They are instantly recognizable, they have millions of fans and they love to collaborate with brands. Celebrities can be used both for advertising and PR communications strategies. This is why the PR department will try to send gifts to celebrities or offer to give them a dazzling outfit for a night out on the red carpet and ensures that their product gets seen and talked about.

In the case of advertising, the celebrities are featured in campaigns and will actively endorse a brand.

How to establish a brand match between celebrity and consumer

Psychological studies (Amos, Holmes and Strutton, 2008) have shown that celebrities have a significant and positive effect on consumers which benefits the brand.

1) Consumers want to emulate the celebrity
2) Consumers believe the testimonial by the celebrity
3) Consumers can memorize the advertisement much better when there is a celebrity
4) Consumers associate the positive traits of the celebrity with the product (but when it backfires, they will also associate the negative traits with the product)

How is a celebrity interesting to a fashion brand? Here is a list of characteristics a fashion brand might be looking for when it wants to do business with a celebrity:

Celebrity career
Has the celebrity had a shiny career with great achievements?

Celebrity scandals
Has the celebrity been involved in any scandal that generated negative press? If so, the consumers might associate the advertised product with the negativity of the celebrity.

Celebrity validity
Would consumers trust this celebrity as an opinion leader on the particular product?

Celebrity authority
Is the celebrity an opinion leader or considered an expert in this area?

Celebrity looks
In a world where good looks can sell a product, it is important that the celebrity is considered to be attractive amongst the target customers.

Celebrity recognition
Will consumers easily recognize the celebrity?

Celebrity/product harmony
Is the celebrity the right fit to endorse a product? Will they be in harmony?

Celebrity endorsement portfolio
Does the celebrity endorse other brands? If so, would they be a competitor? Is the celebrity endorsing too many brands so that the impact is diffused?

Here is a basic compatibility model that can help to establish a perfect match for collaboration:

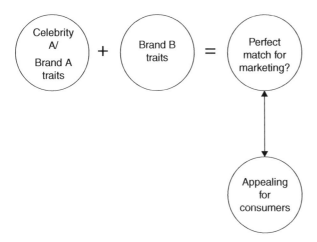

Figure 5.4 Compatibility model for celebrity and brand. Author's original illustration.

Case example: Tod's or the living dead

One interesting way brands use celebrity endorsement is when they work with a famous person who has passed away a long time ago. Nobody would be surprised to see famous icons and movie stars such as Marilyn Monroe, Audrey Hepburn, Frank Sinatra or Einstein – just to name a few.

What are the brand benefits? All the above-mentioned positive effects can be triggered, as global consumers will recognize a star who is still an opinion leader and someone to emulate due to their legendary life. The celebrity shines a positive aura on the product.

Tod's is a brand who played with this type of endorsement a few years back, in the 1990s: They featured Audrey Hepburn, the Kennedys and Grace Kelly in their print campaigns. The celebrities were shown in a black and white original photo that was positioned above a pair of Tod's loafers at the bottom of the page. The consumers were to believe that these celebrities all wore Tod's loafers.

However, only Hepburn and Grace Kelly were wearing loafers in those photos, the Kennedys were barefoot, but that was not even the problem. The problem was simply a matter of chronology, which might only occur to people who know that Tod's was founded in 1978, very much in contrast to the celebrity photos. The photo of Audrey Hepburn is from her film "Funny Face" from 1957, John F. Kennedy only lived until 1963 and Grace Kelly's photo is from a promotional shot from the 1950s film "To Catch a Thief". To put it another way: During their lifetime, none of these celebrities could have possibly worn Tod's loafers from the future and the loafers that they wore in the photos were of course from a different brand. In fact, Audrey Hepburn wore loafers by Salvatore Ferragamo in "Funny Face", and Grace Kelly wore Weejuns Penny Loafers by G.H. Bass & Co., which first came onto the American market in 1936.

In this case, the celebrity endorses a product without his or her consent and the public is led to believe that the brand was truly worn by them. Is it legal? It can be, if all legal aspects are cleared.

What is the downside to this? According to Ad Age "dealing with estates of departed icons and the parties related to their image and product – movie studios, music license holders and the like – can be fraught with complexity that sometimes ends in litigation" (Muratore, 2014).

Ethical considerations

How can consumers distinguish between a blogger's real opinion and an endorsed or sponsored opinion? Should consumers have a clear understanding of the difference?

Working with selected opinion leaders who are groomed by brands to endorse a certain product or service leaves many questions open: Are consumers aware that the opinion leader is being paid for the promotion? When is the opinion leader actually expressing a true personal opinion as opposed to a paid-for-opinion that is likely not genuine? It is therefore very important to make this distinction clear to the consumer so that the consumer can develop an informed decision.

The same is true for celebrity endorsement. There are many cases where a celebrity endorsed a brand but it later became evident that the celebrity has completely different values and the ethics of brand and celebrity do not match. Although this might work at first for marketing measures, once the consumer realizes that the celebrity has a different opinion, this can create disbelief, break of trust and frustration.

The regulations and laws on this are generally vague and give opportunities to mislead the consumer.

The other question is whether an opinion leader or celebrity carries any responsibility for the effects of their endorsement, just like advertisers do. Could their endorsement be potentially harmful to the masses? Would it diminish their self-esteem and self-perception? What if children follow the celebrity through social media and as a vulnerable group are exposed to the same messages? These and more questions need to be considered when approaching marketing through the means of endorsements, influencers and opinion leaders.

Another aspect of celebrity culture is our obsession with it and the arguably unhealthy implications for our psychological and emotional well-being, our self-perception and self-confidence. Clinical psychologist Michael S. Levy (2015) suggests that we have become addicted in a way similar to how someone becomes addicted to drugs or alcohol. If this is true, then a brand which cooperates with celebrities and uses them for endorsements is actually fuelling the addiction and causing harm to society.

Further reading

Bartlett, D. (2013) *Fashion Media: Past and Present*. London: Bloomsbury Academic.

Briggs, M. (2016) *Journalism Next: A Practical Guide to Digital Reporting and Publishing*. 3rd revised edn. Thousand Oaks and London: Sage Publications Inc.

Church Gibson, P. (2011) *Fashion and Celebrity Culture*. Oxford: Berg Publishers.

Cope, J. and Maloney, D. (2016) *Fashion Promotion in Practice*. London: Bloomsbury.

Elihu, K. and Lazarsfeld, P. F. (2005) *Personal Influence: The Part Played by People in the Flow of Mass Communications*. London: Routledge.

Ferragni, C. (2013) *The Blonde Salad. Consigli di stile dalla fashion blogger più seguita del web* (Italian). Mondadori.

Fuchs, C. (2013) *Social Media: A Critical Introduction*. London: Sage.

Gelardi, P. and Barberich, C. (2014) *Refinery29: Style Stalking*. Kindle edition.

Houghton, R. (2012) *Blogging for Creatives*. London: Ilex Press.

Katz, E., Lazarsfeld, P. F. and Roper, E. (Foreword) (2005) *Personal Influence: The Part Played by People in the Flow of Mass Communications*. New York: Free Press.

Lazarsfeld, P. F., Berelson, B. and Gaudet, H. (1944) *The People's Choice: How the Voter Makes Up His Mind in a Presidential Campaign*. New York: Columbia University Press.

Levy, M. S. (2015) *Celebrity and Entertainment Obsession: Understanding Our Addiction*. Lanham, MD: Rowman & Littlefield Publishers.

Pringle, H. (2004) *Celebrity Sells*. Wiley.

Schuman, S. (2009) *The Sartorialist*. Harmondsworth, UK: Penguin.

Tungate, M. (2012) *Fashion Brands: Branding Style from Armani to Zara*. London: Kogan Page.

Van Dijck, J. (2013) *The Culture of Connectivity: A Critical History of Social Media*. Oxford: Oxford University Press.

Target market and segmentation

6

Chapter topics

Do you need a target market?

If you take any fashion brand and pick out their core product, think about who they should sell it to.

The entire world? A few continents? One country? Perhaps the customers are young, single and affluent people who live in metropolitan cities? Or perhaps the product is suitable for the countryside and only for consumers over 50? The constellations are endless and a brand essentially has two choices: Mass-marketing or target-marketing.

With mass marketing no effort needs to be made to figure out which people might or might not buy the product and the brand's communication approach is to tailor one message to all. This can work especially well with staple products such as basic socks, basic underwear, the cotton t-shirt (think Hanes, Fruit of the Loom or Marks & Spencer's) because – one might argue – everyone will need these items in their lives, no matter who they are. In this case, to boost a bland staple product, differentiate the brand from its competitors and reach a mass market, collaborations between brands can be very useful, as was done in the case of H&M who collaborated with David Beckham for their underwear.

With target marketing a brand makes an effort to narrow down and pin-point their customer. This requires market research and segmentation of the market but promises to be less wasteful in terms of resources and more profitable if done correctly.

According to Jackson and Shaw (2009, p.53) "Understanding how a market is segmented makes it easier to plan marketing strategies, to target consumers and position products more accurately".

What that means in reality is that segmentation is a powerful tool which gives a brand competitive advantage over others and is the first stepping stone in the STP Approach: Segment, Target, Position the brand. In terms of the marketing planning, brands are then able to predict consumer behaviour and "develop marketing campaigns and pricing strategies to extract maximum value from both high- and low profit customers" (Rigby, 2015).

Thus, once the segmentation has taken place the brand is aware of its target market or markets and can approach them directly in a way that works best. This is highly important for creating brand communication in the form of advertising and public relations. A brand can only reach its consumer successfully if it speaks his or her language in terms of interests, preference, attitudes and other significant factors.

Case example: Victoria's Secret and Agent Provocateur

Looking at a staple in everyone's wardrobe, who could be the target customer of Victoria's Secret underwear? And who of Agent Provocateur? Both labels sell underwear and the brands are both available online as well as in many global fashion capitals, but their consumers are very different ones.

Victoria's Secret was founded in 1977 by Roy and Gaye Raymond in the USA as a counterweight to boring lingerie and has grown to a large-scale brand available globally, moving into the UK over the last years.

The *Guardian* describes the types of current customers one might encounter in Central London's Bond Street flagship store of Victoria's Secret, which opened in 2012: "The shoppers are a mix of teenage girls with Topshop bags and tourists having their photos taken [...]" (Carter-Morley, 2012).

Victoria's Secret Angels are part of the brand DNA and are slim models of the famous runway carnival-like show. They are all in their 20s, except for an occasional few in their 30s and most VS promotional campaigns are youthful, playful and show happy girls. The brand is not known for high quality but rather the opposite, paired with an affordable price. Despite much controversy which has been surrounding the well-being of the so-called "Angels" who walk in the shows, they remain role-models of young girls and are used in communication campaigns of the brand.

Meanwhile luxury lingerie label Agent Provocateur, which was founded in London by the son of Vivienne Westwood and his wife in 1994, is a brand that "is confident, sensual and irreverent. [Known] for [...] craftmanship, fit, our use of beautiful fabrics and our playfulness" (AP blog). Over the years, it has grown from one small shop in London's raunchy Soho to a global presence. In 2015, the brand used Naomi Campbell in their promotional campaign at the age of 44, set in glamorous pictures of a dark nature with a femme fatale set in crime scenes reminiscent of David Lynch's "The Lost Highway" and Brian de Palma's "Body Double". It is targeted at a far more kinky, luxurious and perhaps mature customer.

According to Martin Bartle, Global Communications and Ecommerce Director of Agent Provocateur, there is an in-house data warehouse which automatically flags customers by value segment, regency, frequency and type of interaction. This information is later used to determine communi-cation strategies with the customers (Dynamic Action, 2015). It is probable that a typical Agent Provocateur customer would not purchase Victoria's Secret lingerie and vice versa as there is a stark difference in disposable income, age, interests and aspirations. Both brands understand how their customers think and target them accordingly. However, Victoria's Secret has been highly scrutinized for promoting unhealthy beauty standards and targeting vulnerable girls whilst Agent Provocateur's raunchy campaign material was not left without stark criticism.

How to segment a market

Generally speaking, there are many ways in which a market can be segmented and for the purpose of this book the standard approaches are discussed along with rarer ones, which are all relevant to the fashion industry. In order to segment a market, first quantitative and qualitative data has to be collected and evaluated. This can be done by using government census data, surveys and questionnaires, data from point-of-sale at the store and e-commerce data, GPS data, customer feedback and focus groups. When you are doing market research you want to be able to have precise information on the demographics, geography, psychographics, purchase behaviour of your customer as well as distribution, time, price and media.

1. Demographic segmentation

What is demography? According to Merriam-Webster it is "the statistical study of human populations especially with reference to size and density, distribution, and vital statistics".

This is a standard way of segmenting the market when people are grouped together based on their age, income, education level and housing type and sometimes their ethnicity. Consumers are also grouped by their gender, but in the fashion world of the twenty-first century, the topic of gender can be of particular interest. With trans-gender models on the catwalks and genderless fashion brands, this can be an effective segmentation tool all by itself.

In 2015, London's Selfridges department store cleverly used the topic of genderless fashion when it opened pop-up areas on their shop floors which offered unisex clothing by leading designers such as Nicola Formichetti's Nicopanda or Ann Demeulemeester.

As the Mailonline reported, the space was "devised by renowned designer Faye Toogood, [and] is an environment in which shoppers are given the freedom to transcend notions of 'his' and 'hers', as you simply find your most desired item by colour, fit and style" (London, 2015).

Popular terminology used in segmenting is via generational segmentation, which includes the terms Generation X, Y, Millennials and Z as well as several more. The consumers are grouped together based on their generations and are given attributes which supposedly apply to all of them to the same degree. And although this type of segmentation is loved in marketing and featured in every marketing book, it must be critically noted that it is not a scientific way of segmenting people. The terms themselves were often coined by journalists or invented by Americans such as researchers Strauss and Howe who mostly focused on the USA. (They invented the Strauss-Howe generational theory.) Thus these marketing generations are often criticized by academics for lack of extensive empirical evidence, for generalizing and being inaccurate.

The generations are as follows:

Lost Generation – born approx. between 1883 and 1900, participated in WWI.
G.I. Generation (or WWII Generation) – born approx. between 1900 and late 1920s, participated in WWII.

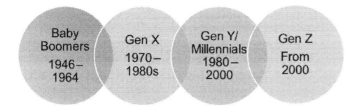

Figure 6.1 Generational segmentation. Author's original illustration.

The Silent Generation – born approx. between the late 1920s and before 1946.

Baby Boomers – born approx. between 1946 and 1964, part of the post-war baby-boom.

Gen X – born approx. between 1970 and early 1980s.

Gen Y – often referred to as Millennials – born between 1981 and 2000. They have many other names such as Generation Me, Echo Boomers, iGen and are a promising new breed of consumers for marketers. This term "Generation Y" was first used in the magazine *AdAge* in the early 1990s.

Gen Z – born from the turn of the millennium (2000) and ongoing. Sixteen years later, there is hardly any information on this group or any idea which one might follow.

2. Geographic segmentation

What is geography? Geography is "a science that deals with the description, distribution, and interaction of the diverse physical, biological, and cultural features of the earth's surface" (Merriam-Webster).

Geographic segmentation thus means that people are segmented by continents, hemispheres, countries, cities or urban, suburban and rural areas, north vs. south or coast vs. inland. For fashion brands this can have high importance because there is a great difference in the fashions worn globally, based on location, climate, cultural, religious, political and ethical factors.

The dictionary's definition mentions culture, which is an element inadvertently connected to geography as regions even within the same country can have clear differences.

For example, urban areas tend to be more extravagant when it comes to experimentation with fashion in comparison with rural areas. An interesting example is how Western fashion brands market to Muslim countries by advertising the same clothing (often shot during the same campaign) but covering up the models. In China, Zara's clothes are associated with Western luxury fashion and reportedly cost up to 90 per cent more than in Spain, whilst in Japan, Western premium and luxury fashion brands and leather goods have a considerable mark-up partly due to high import tariffs and positioning strategies.

In Japan, a consumer gets charged with 30 per cent duty on a pair of boots and then slammed again with a consumption tax of 8 per cent to give a grand total of 38 per cent on a product. "Tariffs such as this imposed on leather items are imposed to make them more expensive than domestically-made leather items" (Higgins, 2015).

A brand might sometimes choose to change the name of the same product when it is sold in different regions such as Mazda's MX5 Miata, which also sported the names Mazda Miata, Mazda MX-5, Eunos Roadster and Mazda Roadster around the world.

And when it comes to language, the same item of clothing might be called by a different name, such as pants in the USA and trousers in the UK (unless you are speaking of underwear).

Geodemographic segmentation is a further development of regional categorization of consumers, for example matching customers' postcodes with their profiles.

According to Jackson and Shaw (2001), the ACORN classification system is widely used in the UK. ACORN stands for A Classification Of Residential Neighbourhoods and was developed by CACI Ltd.

According to the ACORN user guide it "segments households, postcodes and neighbourhoods into 6 categories, 18 groups and 62 types. […] By analysing significant social factors and population behaviour, it provides precise information and an in-depth understanding of the different types of people". acorn.caci.co.uk/downloads/Acorn-User-guide.pdf

1   Affluent Achievers – A Lavish Lifestyles, B Executive Wealth, C Mature Money
2   Rising Prosperity – D City Sophisticates, E Career Climbers
3   Comfortable Communities – F Countryside Communities, G Successful Suburbs, H Steady Neighbourhoods, I Comfortable Seniors, J Starting Out
4   Financially Stretched – K Student Life, L Modest Means, M Striving Families, N Poorer Pensioners
5   Urban Adversity – O Young Hardship, P Struggling Estates, Q Difficult Circumstances
6   Not Private Households – Not Private Households

As an example, let's look at the large category number 3: ACORN states that 40 per cent has a mortgage, 51 per cent are married, 44 per cent have no credit card and 20 per cent are interested in gardening. In category 5, 18 per cent are lone parents, 54 per cent live in socially rented accommodation, 41 per cent pay no tax and 13 per cent are non-white.

3. Psychographic / Lifestyle segmentation

First, let's find out what the term "psychographic" actually means.

According to the   it is "the study of customers in relation to their opinions, interests, and emotions". And if mixed together with their values, attitudes and lifestyle you get quite a life-like portrait of your customer. In fact, psychographic and lifestyle are terms which are often interchangeable.

In order to assess the opinions, interests and attitudes of consumers and then categorize them, qualitative research is conducted by interviewing individuals or groups (so-called "focus groups") and paying close attention to interests, opinions and attitudes voiced. The more customers are questioned the more accurate and representative the results are. The qualitative research can be conducted in person or via telephone, e-mail/internet or even via "snail mail".

For research in fashion, qualitative analysis can be varied and includes straight-forward product-based research as well as cultural or sociological elements.

Over the last decades many marketing research companies have offered their help in customer segmentation by each developing a unique segmentation tool. There is the VALS tool by SRI International, PRIZM by Nielsen or Sinus by Sinus-Institut (the latter mostly used for the German market) The segmentation tools group people together into categories by using quirky names and adding engaging stories. Nielsen as an example has opposing social categories called "Blue Blood Estates" (wealthy, older, with kids) and "Shotguns and Pickups" (white, poor, with rifles, children and trailers) (Claritas, 2015), whilst Sinus Milieus has a category called the "Adaptive Pragmatist Milieu", which is "The ambitious young core of society with a markedly pragmatic outlook on life and sense of expedience: success oriented and prepared to compromise, hedonistic and conventional, flexible and security oriented" SINUSMarkt- undSozialforschungGmbH, 2015).

Scholars and critics often voice their concerns about these segmentation tools for several reasons: The tool are usually trademarked and are aggressively marketed like any other product. This means that they are biased by the wish of financial gain by the proprietors. Second, most of the marketing research companies do not lay open their method of data collection or evaluation which makes it unscientific in any academic circles. Third, consumer groups tend to change their attitudes, which can make the tools outdated. Finally, they are prone to stereotyping humans in a negative way through categories such as race and ethnicity. Sinus Milieus for example offers a separate psychographic category chart for pure Germans (both parents must be of German descent) and another one for all other Germans with a "migration background" (the person, or at least one parent are not of ethnic German descent and have migrated to the country after 1949), the latter of which makes up about 20 per cent of the country's population. Or to put it in other words, every third person with a migration background has lived in Germany since his or her birth but is to be treated differently in marketing terms. Although market segmentation tools can be very helpful it is vital to question its ethics and remain critically observant to how one treats fellow humans.

One typology tool which fashion brands like to use are the so-called pen portraits. The pen portrait uses a fictional person and gives a profile of the person's appearance, lifestyle and attitudes. It will also give specific facts or hard variables such as age, income and social status. Ideally, primary research and qualitative gathering of data will inform the pen portrait and make it more accurate.

There is a closer look at pen portraits in the media segmentation section below.

4. Purchasing behaviour

This area of customer segmentation groups people according to the occasion, benefits sought, usage rate, brand loyalty level, readiness and reason to purchase. Furthermore, the user status can be differentiated: potential, first-time, regular, etc.

Occasions: holidays and events that stimulate purchases. For example, a customer might regularly purchase staples such as underwear and socks and will be loyal to a brand that has provided products with the benefits sought such as comfort, style and price. Whereas the acquisition of an expensive designer handbag might be tied to an occasion such as a birthday or a promotion and will require high involvement in terms of the purchase decision and the careful selection is tied to an anticipated status symbol.

5. Distribution

Here we look at the distribution channels of a product. For example, some premium or luxury designer brands in Europe choose to sell in their own flagship stores, at the airport in the duty free sections as well as in outlet stores (Bally) – each time at different price points. Other brands like Chanel will never discount their products to more than 30 per cent off during sales and are strictly available in their own stores as well as a few selected luxury retailers. However, fast fashion accessories brand Accessorize can be found at train stations, as concession shops within department stores and as stand-alone stores.

With the increasing importance of online channels, many brands are also distributed via e-commerce. Other brands develop their own apps for all available mobile devices and advertise in third-party apps.

For luxury brands, the distribution channel is strictly controlled to ensure scarcity and e-commerce might be restricted or sometimes not available at all. At this price segment, the prestigious store and retail experience is part of the exclusive price that is being paid.

6. Media

Media is crucial for the marketing communications strategy: Which media does the target market turn to and how engaged are they?

The consumers can be reached through a variety of media channels so it is important to segment them by the media they use. According to Kantar (2019) the penetration of internet usage in the UK is 78 per cent.

As mentioned previously, media data which magazines and papers provide can be very helpful for matching up the consumer and the preferred media.

For example, *Grazia UK* has a description (like a pen portrait) of its typical reader who is a woman between the age of 25–45 and more AB profile readers than *Vogue* and *Elle*.

> She's a savvy, affluent, confident, busy and modern woman who actively participates in the world around her. She comes to *Grazia* for edited choice – on everything from the news she needs an opinion on that week to issues she wants to be moved by to simply discovering which heels will instantly make her wardrobe rock. She happily admits she's "addicted" to *Grazia's* unique mix of news, views and shoes.

This description would be a perfect example of a pen portrait which was mentioned earlier. According to Jackson and Shaw (2011), retailers might use pen portrait descriptions of their typical customers to help their design team as well as their retail buyers to better understand and target the consumer.

Note the "AB profile readers", which is based on the NRS social grades system, a classification which is used in the UK. Originating from the world of media and the National Readership Survey to classify readers, this grading is now often used for general marketing and became a staple in Britain, since its invention in the 1950s. It classifies social grade based on occupation.

The National Readership Survey (2015) classification of social grade is as follows:

A   Higher managerial, administrative and professional – (4% of population)
B   Intermediate managerial, administrative and professional – (23% of population)
C1 Supervisory, clerical and junior managerial, administrative and professional – (27% of population)
C2 Skilled manual workers – (21% of population)
D   Semi-skilled and unskilled manual workers – (16% of population)
E   State pensioners, casual and lowest grade workers, unemployed with state benefits only – (9% of population)

(Grazia, 2018)

7. Time

Time segmentation is rare, but might be highly effective for certain brands and markets. This is the case for products which are marketed along with the changing seasons, holidays and special events (remember all the royal paraphernalia for each royal life-time event, such as special biscuit tins to commemorate the birth of Prince George?) or the Olympics. In terms of department stores, time segmentation can relate to increased opening hours and in-store promotions.

8. Price

Although income levels are determined when the demographics are evaluated, a pr icing strategy on its own can help a brand to better reach their target market. In fact, when a brand is looking to expand its target market, such as in the case of TAG Heuer, it might include cheaper products into their range and thus facilitate entry-level products for their new target customers. The brand will be discussed further on in this chapter.

Table 6.1 Summary table with overview of most important segmentation criteria and how a company might access it.

Demographic Includes all facts about a person which might also be available from census data.	Age: From 0 to 100, as this depends on brand
	Generation: Baby-Boomers, Gen X, Y, Z etc.
	Sex: Female, Male, and in fashion gender-neutral, transgender etc.
	Family size: from 1 to open end
	Family life stage young, single, married, no children, youngest child younger than 6, youngest child older than 6, married, separated, widowed, divorced, etc.
	Income: Personal income, household income, for children: caretakers' income, gross income or net income, disposable income, etc.
	Occupation: Working, unemployed, self-employed etc.
	Education: No formal education (this can also apply to children), school, high-school, some college, university (BA/ MA), PhD; apprenticeship
	Social class: lower class, middle class, upper class; possibly terms such as working class, bourgeoisie, aristocracy, etc.
Geographic: All data available on geographic region and its natural as well as cultural factors.	Region: Segmented by continent, hemisphere, country or union of states (i.e. EU, CIS), Inhabitants, population density
	Inhabitants, etc.
	Population density: Often classified as urban, suburban or rural (or rural vs. metropolitan) and segmented by location and population density.
	Climate: Segmented by impact of climate on population such as seasons (four seasons, opposite seasons, no seasons Mediterranean, Temperate, Sub-Tropical, Tropical, Polar, etc.
Psychographic: Qualitative data on consumer, obtained through a form of survey or questionnaire.	Lifestyle
	Personality
	Activities
	Interests
	Opinions
Purchase behaviour: Qualitative data as well as quantitative data (for example collected through sales data) on a person's purchase patterns.	Benefits sought
	Usage rate
	Brand loyalty
	User status: potential, first-time, regular, etc.
	Readiness to buy
	Occasions: usual purchase or special occasion (such as holidays, events etc.)

(continued)

Table 6.1 (Cont.)

Distribution	Flagship
Usually company-internal data evaluating best possible options.	Stand-alone-store
	Concession
	Department store
	Pop-up store
	E-commerce
	Mail-order
Media	Media type, frequency of use, engagement:
Qualitative data as well as quantitative data.	Printed media
	Digital media
	Mobile media
Time	Seasons
Usually company-internal data evaluating best possible options.	Political and social occasion
	Event (Olympics, a royal wedding or a pre-determined sales day (Single's Day, Black Friday)
Price	Pricing strategy
Usually company-internal data evaluating best possible options.	Discounts
	Promotions

How will the demographics develop in the future and globally?

When segmenting the market, statistics are a sound, empirical method of gathering data for further evaluation. When looking at the global population growth until 2100, it becomes evident that the greatest population increase is predicted for Africa and Asia, respectively.

According to the UN (2017), the world population in 2100 is estimated to be approximately 11.2 billion people.

Primary, secondary, tertiary target markets

After segmenting the market, suitable consumers can be grouped together and a brand can determine its primary, secondary and tertiary target markets.

The primary market consists of 60 to 70 per cent of the total target market, the secondary market consists of 15 to 20 per cent of the total target

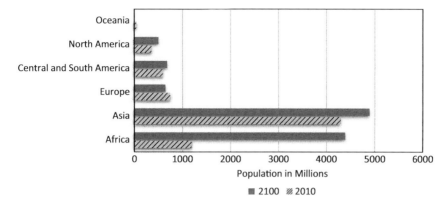

Figure 6.2 Global population growth with a forecast up to 2100. Author's own illustration, based on Statista, 2015.

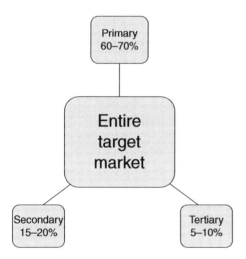

Figure 6.3 Primary, secondary, tertiary target markets. Author's own interpretation loosely based on Bickle, 2010.

market and the tertiary market consists of the remaining 5 to 10 per cent (Bickle, 2011).

Encoding and decoding the brand's message

Once the segmentation has been successfully completed and the target market has been identified, the brand's communication can be tailored to the market.

In terms of advertising and PR, this means communicating the right message through the right channels to the target audience.

A brand might have decided to segment its market and develop a customized marketing programme for their brand communication. There is a clear understanding of who they are targeting with their message and how they'd want the existing and potential consumers to react to it. As they develop the intended message can they be sure that it will be understood?

The theory of message encoding and decoding, first developed by Stuart Hall in the early 1970s, states that the sender encodes the message, sends it through media channels, and the recipient has to decode it or interpret it. Of course the ability to interpret a message is influenced by an individual's culture, background and environment, personal experiences, language and social valances.

Only when the process of decoding has successfully taken place, has the message been truly received. Thus, when creating brand communication, one must ensure that the message is readable for the target recipients.

Whatever the intended message is that the brand has sent, it has no meaning until the recipient has clearly understood it. This sounds very simple and logical, but science reveals that it is not always so obvious. In Figure 6.4 a communication model shows how the meaning of a message is created: The sender, for example a fashion brand, intends to send a message to their target customers, it uses a combination of visual, verbal and non-verbal codes that are supposed to represent their message. It is then sent through a media channel (for example ATL, BTL or celebrity) and arrives at the consumer. The consumer then must be able to decode the cues and finally "gets" the intended message. Only at this very last step will the message actually have created meaning. Fashion, in particular, is built on visual culture, which makes fashion imagery a language of its own. Fashion consumers expect to see messages that use visual language in fashion communication and have learned to decode them over the decades.

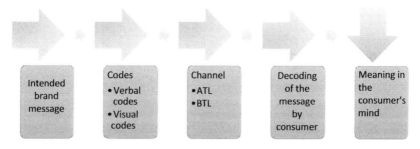

Figure 6.4 Communication model "Coding and decoding of messages". Author's own interpretation, loosely based on Scheier and Held, 2012.

As an example, let's look at watchmakers TAG Heuer who have been trying to target younger customers such as the Millennials (Generation Y) and get them to consider TAG watches as cool and aspirational. Apart from the brand communication, TAG Heuer has also lowered the price for entry level watches to lure in the new target consumers. Furthermore, they have aligned themselves with a popular brand ambassador with 30 million followers worldwide: Their advertising campaign uses visual and verbal codes to encode this particular message by featuring Cara Delevingne – looking standoffish into the camera and showing her wrist with the watch – and the copy text "Don't crack under pressure". The imagery was printed as a classic ATL campaign in fashion magazines seen by consumers, along with social media campaigns, events and other promotions.

Could the target market interpret the intended message correctly? A millennial should be around the same age as Cara and know that she is a star model with a unique personality, described as "the most disruptive It Girl of the moment" (Karolini, 2015).

Furthermore, Cara is a celebrity and trendsetter, so automatically (as discussed in Chapter 4) the recipient trusts Cara's choice of watch. Finally, the verbal cue reveals the added benefit of having such a watch: It helps not to crack under pressure, making you stronger, cooler, more successful (emulation of the star) in any tricky situation.

Behind the scenes, Jean-Claude Biver, President of LVMH Watches and TAG Heuer CEO stated that Cara "matches the brand" and that presently they sell between 35–37 per cent of watches to women, aiming for 50 per cent. "The watch is associate with success. [...] And success is 'don't crack under pressure'. If you crack under pressure you will never be successful".

On their website they describe the brand ambassador:

> From jetsetting off to Paris for a shoot to taking in long hours on film sets, Cara never stops, never settles and fights the constant pressures of being in the spotlight 24/7. This 'it' girl's never dainty, but always sparkling personality was the inspiration for our TAG Heuer Cara Delevingne special edition Carrera 41 MM that's elegant on the outside and unique on the inside with a feminine touch and a killer edge.
>
> She's beauty and the beast all rolled into one exciting package and we can't wait to watch her exciting life unfold.
>
> (www.tagheuer.com/en/cara-delevingne)

How about the technical features of this watch? Do the recipients care about what the Carrera 41 MM model actually does? Imagine TAG Heuer had sent out a different message instead of #DontCrackUnderPressure: Calibre

5 is a self-winding movement with a balance frequency of 28,800 vph (4Hz) and power reserve of 40 to 50 hours. It has push buttons with a black line at 2 o'clock and black line at 4 o'clock. This copy text coupled with a beautiful close-up of the watch itself. No Cara. Could the target audience interpret the intended message correctly?

This is an excerpt from the technical specs, which, unless you are a watch lover or collector, would not mean much to the millennials and most likely the message would be quite meaningless.

Ethical considerations

The main concern of segmentation is the risk of stereotyping, discrimination and stigmatization because segmentation primarily aims to group people together based on pre-determined characteristics and variables, judging them and predicting their behaviour.

The British NRS Social Grade classification system equates occupation to social class, so immediately anyone who works in manual labour is "demoted" to a low social class status. The Sinus Milieus, which hail from Germany, do not include any people who are migrants or the offspring of migrants in Germany. They are not considered to be part of regular society and, in fact, have a separate classification chart.

As history has shown on numerous occasions, any classification of humans is intrinsically flawed and deprives individuals of their dignity and identity, giving way to social injustice. Furthermore, stereotyping encourages prejudice and aggression and even violence.

Classification can be more accurate with the use of big data collection, but this system is also highly flawed and potentially dangerous. One main concern of big data is the collection, use, storage and deletion of it. Website traffic, social networks, mobile applications, forums and blogs and other digital platforms can collect and provide sensitive and detailed information about each individual. For consumers, there is generally very little transparency to the processing and analysing as well as use and transmission of personal data. The ethical question is how data can be collected and processed when it is done so without people's conscious consent (in fact they might not even be aware of this), but at the same time meet legal obligations. If it is artificial intelligence and machines that are used to collect the data, then who programmes and controls them? Finally, the question is what harm can be done with this information, such as targeted discrimination or political and social exclusion? It may be that our technological advances have happened so fast, that people have not caught up with its implications and are lagging behind in regulating it.

Further reading

ACORN acorn.caci.co.uk

Bickle, M. C. (2010) *Fashion Marketing: Theory, Principles, & Practice*. New York: Fairchild.

Dubois, B. (2000) *Understanding the Consumer: A European Perspective*. New York: PrenticeHall.

Jackson, T. and Shaw, D. (2009) *Mastering Fashion Marketing*. Basingstoke: Palgrave Macmillan.

Kawamura, Y. (2011) *Fashion-Ology: An Introduction to Fashion Studies*. New York: Berg.

McDonald, M. (2012) *Market Segmentation: How to Do It and How to Profit from It*. Revised 4th edn. John Wiley & Sons.

Posner, H. (2011) *Marketing Fashion*. London: Laurence King Publishing.

Smith, P. R. and Zook, Z. (2016) *Marketing Communications: Offline and Online Integration, Engagement and Analytics*. 6th edn. London: Kogan Page.

Sociovision/Sinus Milieus www.sinus-institut.de/en/sinus-solutions/sinus-milieus

Nielsen PRIZM www.nielsen.com/content/dam/corporate/us/en/docs/solutions/segmentation/prizm-premier-segments-may-2015.pdf

United Nations (2017) World Population Projected to Reach 9.8 Billion in 2050, and 11.2 Billion in 2100. UN DESA: Department of Economic and Social Affairs. Available at: www.un.org/development/desa/news/population/world-population-prospects-2017.html

Target marketing and the international consumer

7

Coding and decoding brand messages

Chapter topics

A different approach for an international market

We live in a global, interconnected world and many fashion brands expand beyond the domestic market looking for further opportunities, growth and profit. Whether a brand is trying to reach customers in a neighbouring country or whether it is a global player, it will have to consider that there are many different cultures and not all cultures can interpret a brand's message in the same way. What works in the national market might backfire when a brand expands beyond its borders which means that the international market needs to be researched and observed carefully prior to any marketing activity. Believing that your own cultural or ethnic group is superior to that of another – also called ethnocentricity – and relying on consumer behaviour of the brand's native country can lead to crucial mistakes.

The most common challenges are barriers of language, culture and politics that need to be taken into account. A brand has to appraise whether people will understand the message in the same way at all and whether the reaction will even be a favourable one. Encoding and decoding messages becomes a very different task when advertising in foreign cultures.

Intercultural studies have shown that there is significant difference in how people perceive individualism vs. collectivism, masculinity vs. femininity, tendency to avoid uncertainties, national or ethnic identity vs. global identity, religion and many other cultural factors (Müller and Gelbrich 2015).

Example women's rights:

For example, American audiences might be offended by ads which show only men in a stereotypically male situation, expecting political correctness and gender equality. Chinese or Japanese audiences might feel offended about ads that show too much affection between the opposite genders, whereas in some Muslim countries, women must not be shown publicly at all although depictions in advertising might generally be permitted, depending on the strictness of the country. When IKEA published its 2012 catalogue in Saudi Arabia, the omission of all women led to a small scandal, not in Saudi Arabia but on the home turf of Sweden. IKEA had airbrushed all the women out of the catalogue which made government officials in IKEA's native Sweden concerned about the message the company was sending out regarding women's rights. According to Adweek, IKEA issued an apology stating: "We should have reacted and realized that excluding women from the Saudi Arabian version of the catalogue is in conflict with the Ikea Group values" (Cullers, 2012).

Example smells and tastes:

In Japan, people dislike strong perfumes, especially in public places and you will notice that many cosmetics and body care products have no scent or are very lightly perfumed. However, the Japanese love green tea flavour and scent in any food or beverage which is why you will find the western brand Kit Kat in the supermarket with green tea flavour and can enjoy a matcha latte in most cafés.

Example geography:

In Russia, the segmentation criteria of geography is a challenge: There are 11 time zones and the infrastructure for "next-day-delivery" across 17,098,242 sq km of land can be a challenge. More than half of international product purchases stem from major cities such as Moscow and St Petersburg but only 25 per cent of all citizens use the internet for shopping.

Example language:

In terms of language, slogans like "Because you're worth it", which was translated to "Ты этого достоин" / Вы этого достойны in Russia, have caused all emotions from bewilderment to amusement and even criticism by the Church's high patriarch, but did not have the intended effect. This is due partly to the fact that in Russia, the word itself means "virtue", "honour", "nobleness" or "dignity" and as such means the worth of a human. The virtue of a human being is such a deep philosophical, religious and ethical question and with this ad would degrade the worth of a human soul to that of a bottle of cosmetics. So instead of reading "you should have the best beauty cream" (intended message by the western brand) it is decoded as: "You are a horrible person and worth no more than a jar of cream".

Interestingly, when Russian consumers who understand some English realize that a brand has translated a slogan or catch-phrase literally without ever making the effort to find out about the Russian language or culture, they immediately dismiss the brand as ignorant and bad. The risk of losing reputation is great.

Example cultural heritage:

Such was the case when in the 1990s the first McDonald's opened in St Petersburg: Inhabitants of St Petersburg interpreted the choice of location as an insult to their cultural heritage.

McDonald's chose to open shop in a historical building on the famous Nevsky Prospekt, a street which has been featured in classic literature and is similar to the Champs Elysées of Paris and is valued due to the pre-revolutionary architectural masterpieces (most are monuments). The fast-food restaurant was put in lieu of the historical "Café du Nord", a restaurant. A St Petersburg resident recalls: "All of the beautiful Art Deco interiors had been brutally stripped out. Everyone felt offended by the Americans who were tactless and uneducated to put their bistro – which makes two pieces of bread with a meat patty – in a building full of cultural significance". (The café now operates again as Café du Nord 1834.)

Figure 7.1 Nevky Prospekt / Невский Проспект in St Petersburg, Russia. Image source: Pixabay by mobinovyc.

And the residents can get quite serious: According to *Pravda* newspaper, in 1998, a small bomb exploded at an unfinished McDonald's restaurant in St Petersburg because the restaurant's construction was opposed by residents of buildings that were razed to make way for it (*Pravda*, 2007). Says a St Petersburg resident: "Everyone was laughing at McDonalds and were thinking: Serves you well for appropriating our building".

Some 20 years later, political friction is said to have been the reason for the closure of ten McDonald's restaurants in the summer of 2014 in Russia, supported by a decision made by the public health watchdog Rospotrebnadzor who found problems with sanitary violations.

Example language:

In China, the language is based on the system of logograms rather than sounds (phonetical language) and each Chinese character represents a monosyllabic Chinese word or morpheme and there are more than 20,000 characters in a Chinese dictionary.

The CCPIT Patent and Trademark Law Office explains the challenges for brands venturing into China:

> When entering the Chinese market, a foreign company, besides application for the registration of its Latin trademark in China, needs to design the corresponding Chinese trademark and apply for its registration […] Due to the complexity of Chinese language, many foreign companies may have doubts in translating their Latin trademarks into corresponding Chinese trademarks and protecting the Chinese trademarks.
>
> (Wang, 2016)

Western brands have the choice of either translating the brand name into Chinese (this keeps the meaning of the brand name), using transliteration (stays close to original phonetic pronunciation but does not necessarily keep the meaning) or using their western name and logo in the hope that it will gain recognition. The ideal version is when brands create a new brand name which sounds like the original and retains the original meaning (Müller and Gelbrich, 2015).

For example, in terms of favourable transliteration, "Armani" has become "阿玛尼" ("A MA NI"), "Chanel" was changed to "香奈儿" ("XIANG NAI ER"), and "Lancome" to "兰蔻" ("LAN KOU"). "All the selected Chinese characters are related to beauty, elegance, poetry, flowers, perfume, etc., similar to the Latin trademarks in pronunciation, and easy to read. At the same time, these characters, as a whole, are not ready words or phrases with specific meaning.in the dictionary" (Wang, 2916).

Mercedes Benz is a company which achieved the creation of a brand name with a suitable meaning, sound and phonetical length when it translated its name to "ben-chi" (奔驰). This quite suitably means to gallop (or run faster) and thus offers a near-literal translation of the brand and what it represents. However, before it invented "Ben-chi" it reportedly had a translation glitch when it used "ben-si", which has a negative and morbid connotation.

Furthermore, the Chinese culture dates back some 4000 years and permeates the modern-day citizens. This is evident in the mixed significance attributed to conforming with tradition and becoming more "Western". Brands which understand this as a fundamental need of the Chinese consumer have a greater chance of winning their support.

Case example: The Pretenders: a look at pseudo-international brand names

Superdry is a fashion brand with a logo that features Roman letters and the Japanese Kana und Kanji alphabets – they are two of the three alphabets commonly used in the Japanese language. If you wanted to use the logo to figure out where the brand is from, you would be faced with quite a challenge.

Yes, the three Superdry founders really have been to Japan (so this part is true) at some point in the past, but they never lived there, they are not from Japan, they do not even speak "Nihongo" (Japanese language in Japanese). They did, however, fall in love with things like the Asahi Super Dry beer and many other products which claim to be "super"-something. This led the founders to start a fashion label based in the small British town of Cheltenham, which is not very exotic I would say.

Still, in Europe and the USA, the brand Superdry has gained immense popularity with its Japanese-inspired printed clothing and brand name. But what exactly does this Japanese combination of letters mean? When you read Superdry's famous graphics 極度乾燥(しなさい) you hear "Kyokudo Kanso (shinasai)" which can be translated to something like "Extremely dry (do it now)" – and it is not a polite request at all, but rather an order which parents might give to children.

Even though the founders of the brand admitted nonsense wording in 2011, the brand continues to grow and has not deterred its fans in the slightest. This is because in the West Japanese-made goods are considered superior, cool and different and the typeset is a powerful USP which is instantly recognizable. The *Branding Journal* reasons: "Research has shown that European consumers aspire and exhibit inclination towards Japanese brands and this is reflected in their purchase decisions. Moreover, packaging/products scripted in Japanese tend to exude a certain degree of quality and 'wow' factor in the customer's perception" (Ryan, 2016).

To put it briefly: European consumers cannot decode the writing literally but more importantly they decode it as cool.

Interestingly, or perhaps logically, there is not one Superdry store in Japan (last updated in 2015). This is, however, a strategic step by the brand, as Japanese people would not know what they are supposed to think of the phrase of "Jinglish" – a mix of Japanese and English. In fact, in Japan the popular items are t-shirts with English or French prints and fashion brands which sound Wwestern – the exact opposite of Superdry's appeal in the West because consumers love brand names that sound western, regardless whether they are imports or domestic ones. You will find many brand names that are made out a combination of Japanese and English. They sound almost authentic, these supposedly western brands which are called Dainy by JURIANOJURRIE or YUMMY MART by PEACH JOHN, Delyle NOIR as well as Ober Tashe. These are just some of the labels which are on offer in one of the most famous department stores in Tokyo, the Shibuya 109 – or "Ichi-Maru-Kyu" as the locals call it by spelling out the number. This is a fashion mecca for lovers of J-Fashion where young and fashion-conscious people flock in search of fashion styles like "Kawaii" (= super cute), "Gyaru" (super girly) or "oshare" (highly fashionable).

And just like the exotic names of the aforementioned fashion brands, customers also love t-shirts with prints in "Jinglish": "World Difference Execute" or "Trusting To Luck". "Everything is in your hand" or "Much Like Hold" they read. The English-inspired prints are not limited to shirts nor to Tokyo, but you can find them on all sorts of products (chocolate, cosmetics, bath essences etc.) and all over the country.

As in the case of Superdry, the attraction of an imported and superior brand is conveyed by means of a foreign name on the product. The customer transfers these characteristics onto the pretend-brand – irrespective of its true qualities. This smart marketing move can work well for selected brands.

Working with unfamiliar territories

First of all, working with unfamiliar territories and unpredictable customer responses calls for an extension of the communication model "Coding and Decoding of Messages" to six steps and a feedback loop, thus turning a one-way communication model into a two-way communication model.

If you compare this with the earlier communication model of coding and decoding brand messages, you will see a few differences: The codes are not only verbal and visual codes but also actions taken by the brand. This can be PR, advertising or opening of stores as well as simply entering a new market by placing the products on shelves of other retailers. This is why the point-of-sale is added to the channels in step 3. After the consumer has decoded the message and the meaning of the intended message has emerged in his mind a crucial step follows which is the response of the consumer to the said message. On international turf, this response is so vital for a brand to "make it or break it".

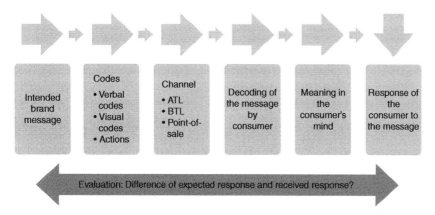

Figure 7.2 Two-way communication model for international markets. Author's own interpretation, loosely based on Scheier and Held, 2012 and Castro and Torch, 2011.

In familiar markets, the worst that can happen is that a consumer only partially understands the message or is simply disinterested. But as we have seen in the preceding examples, in foreign markets the consumer might be repulsed or angered by a brand and he or she will then refuse to accept it. The response of the consumer is critical for the brand and it must evaluate if there is any difference in the response expected and the response received.

This theory of comparing the expected response to the intended response is actually used in the aviation industry, where communication is the key to a successful and safe flight operation. For example, in the cockpit there are constant verbal exchanges between the pilot and co-pilot, as well as air traffic control. In order to ensure that the intended message is received and understood the correct way a system of repetition, verification and control is employed. Oftentimes when aviation accidents happened and the flight deck recording was later examined, there was miscommunication present and thus a human factor responsible for a less than desirable event. According to Airbus, a survey of NASA found 80 per cent of all accidents to have occurred due to incorrect communication with 45 per cent attributed to listening (Airbus, 2004).

For this reason, the so-called Cockpit and Crew Resource Management is a recurrent training factor for aviation professionals. All businesses on the ground can learn from aviation by not only listening to responses from their consumers but also expecting that the response might not be the intended one.

In terms of segmentation, a different approach is also needed for an international market:

Wind and Douglas (2001) have suggested that international markets need to be segmented in two steps: First the country in terms of the macro environment has to be evaluated and then the customer characteristics.

In detail, the recommended segmentation criteria of the macro environment include:

	General country characteristics
	Geographic location
	Demography
	Level of socioeconomic development
	Cultural characteristics
	Political factors
	Economic and legal constraints
	Market conditions
	Product bound culture and lifestyle characteristics

The customer characteristics are based on the same principles as the segmentation mentioned at the beginning of this chapter, including demographics, psychographics and lifestyle data.

Case example: Cadbury Dairy Milk in India

Here is an example of a western brand which cleverly used the knowledge of a foreign market to advertise for chocolate:

> Imagine a tricky social situation, such as a woman in her 50s wearing a pair of jeans for the first time and being too scared to leave her home because all neighbours (and mother-in-law) will judge her negatively. Her husband hands her a small piece of chocolate and this gives her the confidence she needs to step outside her door. Once she does, her neighbours praise her new jeans and all is well.

Most likely, the above scenario makes absolutely no sense to you (unless you are familiar with the Indian culture). Why would a woman in her 50s not wear jeans? Why would neighbours have any right to comment? And why would a small piece of chocolate solve this mysterious emotional trouble?

The answer lies in a commercial that was launched in 2010 by Cadbury Dairy Milk (CDM) and the infamous advertising agency Ogilvy & Mather. This campaign under the name of the "Shubh Aarambh" is based on the concept of the Indian tradition of having something sweet before every auspicious occasion, with the belief that it leads to a favourable outcome.

There are several commercials in the series and Abhijit Avasthi, national creative director, Ogilvy & Mather India, said, "While unfolding the 'Shubh Aarambh' theme, we were consciously looking for situations which have universal appeal, though they might connect a little better with certain age profiles. [...] 'Jeans' might work a little harder with the adults. Other themes that follow will be equally surprising yet real" (Rao, 2010).

Has Cadbury managed to create a brand message which can be decoded by the consumers of that particular culture? This campaign is said to be extremely successful, having replaced traditional Indian sweets with Cadbury's Dairy Milk chocolate at home. Furthermore, Ogilvy & Mather helped to create a campaign which was suitable for television – a very popular medium in India amongst advertisers.

According to Statista (2015), Asia Pacific is the second largest regional advertising market in the world with advertising spending in the region reaching a total of 158.3 billion US dollars in 2015. The growth in the region is mainly driven by China, the world's second largest ad market, and India, one of the fastest growing advertising markets in Asia.

The potential of international markets

With all the challenges given, is it still worth venturing out into the international market? Consider the forecast for the future: The EU and USA are mostly saturated markets with little growth perspectives. However, there are high hopes on the emerging economies of the "BRIC" countries: Brazil, Russia, India, China. And according to Euromonitor (2013), by 2020, China and Russia will displace USA and Germany respectively making the world's largest economies China, USA, India, Japan and Russia.

1. China

This country has seen growth ever since the Special Economic Zones were introduced from 1980. China has cheap and strong labour costs, a growing appetite for consumer goods and fashion as well as many self-made millionaires who love luxury. China now not only produces for export but also for its own consumption and has higher demands by customers than before. China also has the world's largest population.

2. USA

The USA lost a lot of its power during the time of the 2007/2008 crisis and is struggling to regain its balance. With a new presidency from 2017, it remains to be seen if the USA can hold a downward spiral, including a shrinking middle-class, low production and low demand.

3. India

India has a large population and a thriving workforce. Consumers are looking at traditional Indian brands but also at western products, making it a lucrative market. Indian consumers have a long-standing relationship with the concept of luxury and western luxury brands are taking advantage of this by opening stand-alone boutiques as well as luxury shopping malls.

4. Japan

Japan has a serious problem with its demographics as the country sees the oldest population growing and the birth rate declining. Abenomics (アベノミクス Abenomikusu) have not been able to give Japan the desired economic boost, but there is hope because Japan is highly advanced when it comes to technological innovation and perfect engineering. In fact, Japan was rated fourth most innovative country by Bloomberg in 2016.

Japanese consumers love fashion, including luxury fashion, but this is nowhere as strong as it was once in the 1980s where luxury spending was extortionate.

5. Russia

Russia's economic power hails from natural resources, such as oil, gas and precious metal (Alrosa is the world's largest diamond mining company), containing more than 30 per cent of the world's natural resources. It is also an innovative country, ranking 12th on Bloomberg's Innovation Index in 2016. There is increasing wealth amongst the rising middle class alongside with a very high number of billionaires, who have residencies in Moscow and are consumers of luxury goods. The luxury market has survived economic and political sanctions very well.

6. South Korea

South Korea is developing rapidly in terms of economy, technology and fashion, putting itself into high global rankings in all three categories (think K-Pop, K-Beauty and K-Drama). Although Korea exports its own beauty, fashion and pop-culture brands – also known under the term "Hallyu", it is also developing a large appetite for western ones. Chanel took its cruise collection to show in South Korea in 2015. Bruno Pavlovsky, Chanel's head of fashion explained in an interview with Business of Fashion:

> […] Today, South Korea is the most influential country in Asia, with its energy and creativity, its youth culture and the pop music and TV celebrities, who have become incredibly powerful, even in China and Japan. […] South Korea is [also] a fast-growing market, a very interesting one, now also open to the Chinese and Japanese who like to travel here for tourism. South Korea has become a top destination in Asia.
>
> (Longo, 2015)

Lastly, there is a new form of economy on the rise: E-commerce. A report by McKinsey and Altagamma (2015) predicts that by 2025, the online market could grow up to 70€bn, making it the third largest economy in the world after China and the USA.

So there is also huge potential for reaching consumers through e-commerce, especially in the emerging economies. China has now become the world's largest internet market with 721 million users, followed by India with 333 million users and then the USA. If this seems a lot, think again: "a new report released today by the UN Broadband Commission for Sustainable Development also confirms that just six nations – including China and India – together account for 55% of the total global population still offline, because of the sheer size of their populations" (UNESCOPRESS, 15.09.2016).

This shows immense potential for future growth as nearly 50 per cent of the global population can become internet users and future consumers of globally acting brands.

One key factor to successful international marketing for brands is to remain flexible. As Euromonitor reported in 2015: "As in all emerging markets, success is based on knowledge – an understanding of the market, but also the economy, consumers, competitors and suppliers.companies which have been successful in China have managed".

They stress the different attitudes, tastes and motivations of consumers in the east to that of consumers in the north, with coastal cities again being different to those inland (Booumphrey, 2015).

Domestic ethnic advertising

Lastly, there are different ethnicities within one country or region which call for ethnic marketing. This is usually targeted at ethnic minorities who might respond better to being addressed in their native language, with brand communication that understands their values and needs.

Such is the case with fashion and lifestyle magazines which cater to African-American audiences in the USA, or brands such as Khushbu Fashions, a UK-based fashion brand which sells Indian clothing and Pakistani fashion online.

Ethnic marketing is well developed in the USA and the UK, but it is in its early stages in continental Europe. It is, however, a lucrative market in countries where there is a high percentage of ethnicities. In Germany about 20 per cent of inhabitants have a non-German background and ethnic marketing has been tried, however this might prove unlucrative in Japan where around 2 per cent of the population is non-Japanese making it a highly homogenous market. According to the Justice Ministry, the largest groups of non-Japanese nationalities are Chinese, with 665,847 people, accounting for almost 30 per cent of foreign residents in Japan, followed by 457,772 South Koreans and 229,595 Filipinos.

Ethical considerations

Intercultural awareness and sensitivity are indispensable when designing a brand message for a consumer group outside our own comfort zone. The comfort zone might be the domestic market or specific cultures and countries which the fashion brand is well aware of and knows what is considered acceptable and what will offend consumers.

However, outside this zone, the brand can tread in dangerous waters of miscommunication which can easily backfire and even destroy the business, as many have seen with the Dolce and Gabbana case in 2018 in China, when an ad was labeled everything from "provocative" to "racist" to simply "incomprehensible".

One take on a faux-pas such as the one by D&G is ethnocentricity.

Any country can be accused of ethnocentricity. It means "believing that the people, customs, and traditions of your own race or nationality are better than those of other races", but it is not necessarily racist.

Ethnocentric behaviour is therefore not the same as racism or patriotism, although it's often found alongside both of these. Ethnocentricity compares people to outsiders by using the cultural norms of their own group so one can believe that but not act out the sentiment.

However, this can become an instant problem if this is your business attitude. And as we see quite clearly in such cases as D&G's ad for the Chinese consumers, when you are trying to break into a foreign market and appeal to foreign consumers, not researching their mentality meticulously and not respecting their cultural norms, it can become a massive problem. D&G's creative team continued to use the same European, ethnocentric, tongue-in-cheek approach to advertising and brand communication in a very different market, a very different cultural setting and with a big outcry and negative social media storm as a result.

Further reading

Briggs, P. (ed.) (September 2016) The State of Broadband 2016: Broadband Catalyzing Sustainable Development. *Broadband Commission for Sustainable Development.* Available at: www.broadbandcommission.org/Documents/reports/bb-annualreport2016.pdf

De Mooij, M. (2010) *Consumer Behavior and Culture: Consequences for Global Marketing and Advertising.* 2nd edn. Sage Publications.

Matharu, S. (2011) *Advertising Fashion Brands to the UK Ethnic Market: How Ethnic Models influence Ethnic Consumer Purchase Behaviour.* Verlag, Germany: VDM.

Solomon, M. R. (2016) *Consumer Behavior: Buying, Having, and Being.* 12th edn. London: Pearson.

Brand communication at the point-of-sale 8

Sensory branding

Chapter topics

Sensory branding

Sensory marketing and sensory branding try to appeal to all the senses in relation to the brand. It uses the senses to relate with customers on an emotional level and increases brand awareness. Sensory brand immersion also creates an emotional sense of place and promotes brand loyalty. "The term *emotional sense of place* describes the sum of human feelings, which can be evoked by a certain physical location [...] The feelings are based on personal experiences, memories and symbolic meanings which are all connected to the location" (Bischoff, 2006).

Table 8.1   Information transition rates of the senses.

Sensory system	Bits per second
Eyes	10,000,000
Skin	1,000,000
Ears	100,000
Smell	100,000
Taste	1000

Our five senses are made up of visual, auditory, olfactory, gustative and tactile senses and there are various studies which indicate which sense can pick up the most information. One version states that the visual sense – so our eyes – is the strongest, followed by the tactile sense of our skin, the ears, smell and finally taste. Each of the senses absorb around 11 million bites of information per second which directly feed into our subconscious. This is because our conscious mind is only able to process 40 bits of information per second. It is assumed that due to this up to 95 per cent of our purchases are triggered by our subconsciousness.

Furthermore, when activated alone, or together in combinations, the effect on our brain and lasting emotional memory can be quite strong. This is due to the fact that the sensory perceptions are processed in the limbic system of our brain.

One of the oldest examples of sensory branding for commercial purposes is Singapore Airlines appealing to our olfactory sense: SQ started spraying its signature "Stefan Floridian Waters", a mélange of rose, lavender and citrus, on its hot towels more than 30 years ago. The company recently tried applications of the same perfume in a Singapore ticket office. Passengers fondly spoke of a typical Singapore Airlines smell when entering the plane and had pleasant memories of the in-flight experience.

Burberry on Regents Street in London appeals to our sense of taste (and smell) by offering a gustatory experience in its very own Thomas's Café. The menu features everything from Eggs Benedict to Lobster and from Japanese tea from Kyoto to Champage.

Armani has a more Italian approach, which certainly is aligned with the brand's ethos: The Armani Caffé and Restaurants in Milan, Paris, Cannes, Munich, London, Doha, Dubai, Hong Kong, New York and Tokyo. The Dubai Restaurant states: "Savour traditional Italian cuisine and modern interpretations of classic dishes brought to life by signature Armani hospitality. The finest ingredients, accomplished chefs and most authentic of flavours are enjoyed against a stylish, contemporary backdrop" (Armani Hotel Dubai, 2018).

The food's luxury description is almost interchangeable with the description of Armani's luxury fashion and thus is a sensory experience that will make the brand most memorable in the subconscious, probably influencing the next purchase decision.

Confectionery is another popular item: Gucci has Gucci chocolates and Hermès has created an edible Birkin Bag made from chocolate. In China, an emerging economy that is continuously important for the fashion and luxury business, brands are in a race to offer the most beautiful and tasty "Moon Cakes" for the mid-autumn festival. This round pastry is a traditional sweet which luxury houses such as Louis Vuitton, Tiffany, Tod's, Gucci, Armani, Kenzo and Fendi send to high-profile customers and KOL's or Key Opinion Leaders in beautiful boxes.

Communication buildings

"A good building must do two things, firstly it must shelter us, secondly it must speak to us", said Peter Stutchbury (2016), an Australian architect.

A directly operated store and a flagship store especially, can serve as a point of brand immersion and communication with the customer and for such projects, company budgets often invest millions.

One such exemplary communication building is not from the fashion industry but from the automotive industry. The BMW Welt which literally means BMW World in German, is an impressive building and interactive space, which was commissioned by the car manufacturer and opened in 2007. It sits on the outskirts of Munich and attracts up to 25,000 on some days. According to the architectural firm HimmelB(l)au, the space is "where the corporation goes into dialogue with its customers, friends and visitors from all over the world – a place of meeting and of change (…) This means: To see, feel, hear, smell, taste the brands – in brief: To experience the world of the brands of BMW Group with all senses".

In fact, the sensory experience is triggered by a modern, bright and vast space, carefully designed to feature interactive exhibitions, tours, food and drink as well as a dramatic sales platform where the new cars are handed over to the customers in an emotionally charged ritual (customers report of crying when seeing their car for the first time during the ritual). If you describe the space with adjectives and describe the BMW brand with adjectives, you would likely have interchangeable words.

This is a successful example of a communication building from another industry. Can fashion create such spaces, too?

Case example: Hugo Boss flagship store in Tokyo

The menswear flagship store of Hugo Boss in Tokyo is such an architectural and sensory marvel, partly because award-winning architect Norihiko Dan had the task of squeezing it onto a small plot of land and directly within the L-shaped embrace of the concrete flagship store of Tod's. Also known as the Keyaki building, it opened in 2013 and features a structure composed of multiple leaf-shaped columns made from steel reinforced concrete. The concrete columns have a surprising wood-like texture (visible when close), which was developed by pouring concrete into a wooden mould.

The concrete construction stands in the upmarket shopping district of Omotesando where luxury shoppers seek to be entertained by brands. Within the Hugo Boss store, the use of materials such as concrete, wood, textiles, and light and smell (there is a Hugo Boss scented candle) it takes the shopper on a sensory immersion and into the world of Boss.

Within the space of a flagship store, the consumer can experience a brand with all his or her senses and the more positive the experience is, the more positive memories will be created, which can lead to loyalty and brand preference.

Integrating digital technology at the point of sale

Currently customers live in a fusion world of the digital and physical, expecting brands to reach them on all possible channels. Thus it is only natural to offer both worlds inside the store too.

This creates a journey for the customer from the first digital contact on a digital personal device to the physical purchase experience in the store. According to a study by McKinsey & Company (2015) on the digitalization of companies, customers have reported a dramatically better brand experience and engagement.

Some brands that have played with the idea of integrating a digital interface in their store are:

Burberry – Interactive tables, video walls
Prada – Digital changing rooms
Tommy Hilfiger – Augmented reality fashion shows changing rooms
Karl Lagerfeld – Interactive digital tables and mirrors
Zara – RFID technology
Gucci – Digital entertainment for children
Nike – Multi-touch, multi-user wall, smartphone interaction

Figure 8.1 The Hugo Boss Keyaki building (flagship store) in central Tokyo, Japan, which is taller than the L-shaped Tod's flagship store immediately surrounding it. Image kindly provided by Hugo Boss.

Figure 8.2 Inside the Hugo Boss Keyaki building (flagship store) in central Tokyo, Japan. Image kindly provided by Hugo Boss.

Karl Lagerfeld installed ipads inside the changing rooms in the flagship store in Munich, with the intention of inviting the customer to take selfies and upload them on social media, turning the shopper into a brand ambassador. This simple installation creates a buzz around the brand, reaches opinion leaders, helps inter-action of customers and potential customers through social media and ensures harmony of off-line and online communication activities.

The ipad features a photo of Karl behind a camera, seemingly ready to snap your photo. In the new clothes, the customer takes pictures and edits them with frames and decorations. After that, the interface asks to upload the picture onto the Karl Lagerfeld Facebook page.

In summary, the benefits of using sensory branding at the point of sale and in brand communication is:

- Increase of in-store traffic
- Increase of time spent in the store
- Increase of brand awareness
- Customers are connected to social networks
- Increase in sales and revenue
- Repeat sales
- If the store uses technology for stock management, further benefits can be better merchandise and stock-management improving customer service and sales as well as personalized service: Individualization and product adjustments directly in stores.

Sonic branding

How do you make a brand forever recognizable by a jingle? How does a song become a bestseller (perhaps for a second time)? You need to write brand-identifying sounds and put them into commercials and the science behind is sonic branding. Sonic branding builds on the idea of our auditory sense. Many brands have engraved themselves in our memory thanks to recognizable jingles or by using popular songs as their identity. Prime examples are the sound bites electronics and computer operating systems make when you start the device, which uses sound bites that last no more than a few seconds but are instantly recognizable. McDonald's famously aligned itself with Justin Timberlake's song and kept the jingle "I'm loving it" as their brand sound.

But for fashion it is more complex when it comes to creating consumer associations with sound and a jingle hardly suffices.

Fashion brands use longer tracks of music in commercials, from short extracts of well-known songs, to full length compositions accompanying an entire film.

Music in fashion ads can even rise to fame, become a symbol of popular culture and become a hit single for a second time. Such was the case with Levi's when in the late 1990s the brand teamed up with a yellow furry puppet. The hit tune by the French electronic musician and film-maker Quentin Dupieux aka Mr Oizo was used in conjunction with his "Flat Eric" puppet to create an unprecedented fashion ad. The genious behind the ad was advertising legend Sir John Hegarty. But not even Hegarty himself could predict the success of the commercial which seemed a bit odd to the brand's executives at first. But once it was released the popularity was of an explosive nature with fans building fan-sites dedicated to the puppet and requesting Flat Eric merchandise whilst the fictional character rose to cult status. Levis went on to make several more commercials with the yellow puppet, establishing a clear link between commercial fashion and popular culture (Caird, 2016).

Prior to that, Levis had revived Dianah Washington's version of "Mad about the boy", which she sang in 1952. In 2002, Levis used classical music for the first time in their advertising, when with the help of BBH (again) the brand produced a highly expensive commercial using music by Handel. The arranger of the classical piece was John Altman who has scored more than 4000 TV commercials.

The Emmy Award-winning composer, arranger and conductor writes music for films and TV and has won every major creative award, including the inaugural MPA Music in Advertising Award. His compositions for Levi's and Renault won the Campaign Award for Best Soundtracks in 2003 and 2004.

Amongst his commercials for famous fashion brands are Gucci, Wrangler and Prada to name just a few. He scored Ridley Scott's fashion film for Prada, which was released in 2005 at the Berlin Film Festival. It was timed with the launch of Prada's new fragrance and Miuccia Prada asked film director Ridley Scott and his daughter Jordan Scott to create the film project. Jordan wrote the poem, "Thunder Perfect Mind", which deals with the endless aspects of the female psychology.

Interview with John Altman

Figure 8.3 John Altman.

Q: How did you start writing music for TV, film and advertising?

JA: I was in a group called Hot Chocolate, played saxophone, and they weren't happy with the musical arrangements that had been done for them. So I said: "I'll do some if you like". They liked what I wrote and suddenly I was an arranger. And in those day, in the mid-1970s, a lot of the TV arrangers were ex-dance band musicians who looked down on genres like reggae, country & western funk and although I liked all popular music, from the turn of the century almost, I was also conversant with all the other forms of music because I was a young guy. So they would pass it on to me – if they had to do a variety show – any arrangements that were slightly more modern. I started writing for popular television variety shows and about the same time I had started arranging for commercials and records. One day an advertising agency in the Netherlands wanted to use a Beatles song in their commercial, but in those days it was impossible to licence a Beatles track for advertising, so the director said "why don't you write something?" and well, I did and they loved it and that became the music for their campaign. And immediately I was a composer as well as an arranger. Then I started composing for BBC drama and arranging music for other composers in music and a similar thing happened. Somebody said "why don't we get you to write the music and cut out the middle man?" and I became a film composer. This was all happening simultaneously, while I still carried on my career as an arranger with lots of hit records to my credit and as a saxophone player with people like Van Morrison. I was firing on all cylinders!

Q: You have worked on many films such as Titanic and James Bond Golden Eye. Why is it that fashion brands have now turned to films, or rather short films, instead of advertising? Is there something they want to copy from the movies?

JA: Films are a unique combination of visual effects, emotional story lines and impactful music. When we watch a really strong film, it will create a lasting memory in our minds. So I think fashion brands want to tap into this powerful emotional connection with their audience. The element of the script, or the story-telling if you want, is the same for both feature length films and short films, which is exactly what brands today do – they tell compelling stories.

Q: How would you say this story-telling in the short fashion films differs from classic commercials, such as the Levis one where you arranged Handel's music?

JA: The absolute luxury of commercials really is time. You have to tell everything immediately. When you think that the longest TV commercial is going to be 90 seconds and the shortest possibly 10 seconds, you really have to make maximum impact in the short time. With film this gets stretched, so, for example, the film I did for Prada directed by Ridley Scott was 7 minutes long, which is ample time to create a vibe, a general atmosphere which can either focus on one product or many.

Q: With the Prada fashion film, what was the creative process when you wrote the music? How did you interpret the brand's message and how did you translate it into sound?

JA: It had to be stylish, mysterious, timeless and impactful yet fun and playful so in a way very much what the brand stands for. In terms of interpreting – the same process I would use for scoring a full-length feature film. The only difference being 7 minutes which is unusual for a feature film, unless it is for example a chase sequence.

Q: You used a live orchestra to record the soundtrack for the commercial. How do you feel this is more beneficial than using a synthesized track?

JA: The main benefit is the emotional impact you can make by using live musicians that you can't achieve by using machinery. For example, using a muted trumpet with crescendos and diminuendos broadens your emotional palette and also allows the music to breathe.

Q: Fashion films are often filled with a star cast of directors and actors. Who was involved in the Prada one?

JA: There were Jordan & Ridley and the French Director of Photography Philippe Le Sourd.

Miuccia Prada had designed the clothes which the protagonist and supermodel Daria Werbowy wore, styled by Kym Barrett of Matrix. And then there was Tom Foden who has worked with both Ridley & Jordan in the past and came on board as production designer. Blanca Li was the choreographer for the film.

The music was performed by a small jazz ensemble that included Frank Sinatra's bass player of choice Chuck Berghofer, trumpeter Jeff Bunnell, percussionist Tiki Pasillas who features with Marc Anthony (Jenifer Lopez' husband). The drummer is Bernie Dresel from the Brian Setzer Orchestra. It was recorded in LA.

Ethical considerations

A factor to consider are the side effects of sensory branding. The idea of sensory overload is discussed in more detail in Chapter 9. Sensory overload is an over-stimulation of our senses which can have detrimental effects on physical and psychological well-being. It is problematic for people who might have conditions such as a predisposition to seizures, autism and Asperger's syndrome as well as a sensitive nature to stimuli.

In a race to impress the consumer with immersive experiences and take more of the market share, brands become indifferent to the effect of their marketing practices. A high-stimulation place with lots of digital interfaces might also be confusing and unsuitable for children and elderly people.

Gjoko Muratovski (2011) argues that architecture has been used since ancient times as a means of political and religious propaganda, such as ancient Greece, Rome or Egypt where buildings were commissioned to convey the power of the ruler or an empire. In more modern times, the USA, Ex Soviet Union, Berlin and other capitals constructed monumental structures that were 'architectural propaganda'.

However, when brands and not governments transform our landscape, what are they propagating? Our immediate environment is designed and curated by companies with strong commercial interest and in turn propagates consumerism.

When cities no longer represent the fine arts, architecture and urban development but are a playground for the coolest, the loudest, the tallest branded buildings, what meaning of life and which aesthetics do we derive from our surroundings? A museum building, as a contrast, is a cultural space, which is often accessible to all people, most ages and backgrounds (free or for a small fee). Are branded spaces equally inclusive and accessible without the pre-requisite of making a purchase and does it add to the cultural value of a place? (Perhaps this is what cultural space the "Maison LVMH" and the "Fondation LVMH" are trying to achieve.)

Brands thus become responsible for our cultural capital, the heritage of a city and the socio-cultural environment of present and future generations, however, this responsibility towards society is not necessarily compatible with business interests.

Furthermore, big brands and corporations have been known to fuel gentrification. They can drive out small businesses which add to the liveliness and character of a city and might have along-standing heritage. As Naomi Klein already wrote as we entered the twenty-first century, Starbucks had a strategy for taking over urban spaces: The company took over entire neighbourhoods by simultaneously opening several cafés, forcing small and long-established competitors to close. Nearly two decades later, the strategy still very much applies with no large global city left untouched.

Further reading

Ferrari, P. and Rizzolatti G. (eds.) (2015) *New Frontiers in Mirror Neurons Research*. Oxford: Oxford University Press.

Fiore, A. M. (2010) *Understanding Aesthetics for the Merchandising and Design Professional*. New York: Fairchild Books.

Gabay, J. (2015) *Brand Psychology: Consumer Perceptions, Corporate Reputations*. London: Kogan Page.

Hulten, B. (2009) *Sensory Marketing*. New York: Palgrave Macmillan.

Lewis, R. and Dart, M. (2014) *The New Rules of Retail*. 2nd edn. New York: Palgrave Macmillan.

Lindstrom, M. (2010) *Brand Sense: Sensory Secrets Behind the Stuff We Buy*. Revised, updated edn. New York: Free Press.

Minsky, L., Fahey, C. and Kotler, P. (2017) *Audio Branding: Using Sound to Build Your Brand*. London: Kogan Page.

Pelger, M. (2015) *Designing the Brand Identity in Retail Spaces*. New York: Fairchild Books.

A critical look at advertising

9

Brands selling hopes, dreams and objectification

Chapter topics

Why criticize advertising?

Advertising surrounds us everywhere, it informs us about products, entertains us and sometimes irritates us. We think that we know what it is all about and can consciously choose to ignore its influence if we wish to do so. Or do we? A fundamental problem with advertising has been pointed out by many critics, authors and academics: It causes more harm than good to society, it misinforms, it warps reality, it obviously tries to influence and manipulate consumers, and "by the sheer weight of exposure, advertising sets a social agenda of what is expected, what is fashionable, and what is tasteful [...]" (Lane, 2008, p.755). Advertising is more powerful and it is more harmful than we think.

The exposure to ads is inescapable because one cannot un-see or un-hear an ad in most public and private surroundings. As individuals encounter ads, they inadvertently and often unconsciously form a psychological and emotional relationship with them.

Still, many people are in denial of the influences of advertising's "because it is quick, cumulative and for the most part it's subconscious" (Kilbourne, 2010).

Advertising is even more harmful to children and adolescents who are easily influenced and might copy peers or role models they see. In some instances, advertising is blatantly disturbing, such as the case with shock advertising.

However, there are regulations and watchdogs which can step in when advertising goes too far. Also some places have consciously chosen to limit or eradicate advertising in public spaces (and beyond). In all three places, the landscape changes dramatically due to the limit or absence of ads. What is it like to live in a place with no advertising? An interview with a former Soviet movie star gives answers to this question.

The relationship of the self with the ads: hopes, dreams and fears

To understand our relationship with advertising and the influence it has on us, we first have to look at the mutual relationship of the person and the ad. What exactly happens in our minds and which emotions appear when we look at an ad?

Sofia Coppola, who directed the ad for Marc Jacob's fragrance "Daisy" inadvertently explains the mechanism in fashion advertising: "I guess with the fragrance, you imagine the woman you're going to be when you wear it. Part of the experience [...] is that you think about a life you're going to have. That's what fashion is too" (Blasberg, 2014).

There is a relationship that advertising forms with us. Freud's disciples and successful marketers like Bernays or Dichter applied the then new theories of the self and the hidden desires as a clever marketing tool. They believed that each person has hidden dreams, hopes, fears and insecurities deep in their subconscious. They argued that people could be made much more aware of those deep emotions and offered a solution to the problem: buying things.

This worked very well in many instances because people did not realize that the emotions would not subside with the purchase and went shopping to feed their aspirations.

Modern day neuroscience has confirmed what the psychologist Ernest Dichter argued from the 1930s to the 1960s: Purchase behaviour is not conscious. It is not even subconscious but unconscious. Dichter studied the theories of Sigmund Freud in Vienna and fled the growing Nazi regime in the early 1930s. He came to New York and began a new career in marketing which was built on his knowledge of psychoanalysis. It revealed that for customers, objects had the meaning of sex, fear, rewards and prestige. He worked for many companies, including Chrysler and Ivory soap. Dichter infused his marketing and advertising messages with implied meanings: For example, he noticed that people paid close attention to their cleanliness and bathed before a romantic date. So Ivory soap was advertised with copy like "Romance can't be rationed – if you take Baby's Beauty tips!" giving hope to those individuals who were eager for romance. Brands like Ivory had to communicate to our insecure self, to the hopeful self.

Let's look at a technique that was used in the middle of the twentieth century: fear. Fennis and Stroebe (2010) recount a famous ad for Listerine, which used the scary medical term halitosis. Their product, which was originally sold as a surgical disinfectant (for body and floors) made bad breath a socially unacceptable trait and catastrophe for all relationships even though prior to the ad campaigns, society was not self-conscious about it and certainly did not see it as much of a problem. But the ad campaigns aimed at the very nerve of humans which is social exclusion. Halitosis would leave women "Often a Bridesmaid … never a bride" or lonely without any friend but a single bird in a cage. There were many terrifying examples like these in the ads and they all offered a solution, which was the infamous mouthwash. When people watch such ads (and there are many of them even today, using fear as a motivator) they immediately empathize and identify with a person – at least for the duration of the commercial. If the ad resonates with the inner self, the person will also try and imitate to a certain degree.

This is something that neuroscience has supported recently when it found so-called mirror neurons: It is a type of neuron, which is said to fire when a primate sees others in action or does the action himself. For the neuron, there is no difference of whether the action was passive and just an observer or whether we imitated the action. Scientists have argued that this is the neurological function of empathy.

But even without a scientific explanation, we humans have the capacity of imagining ourselves in someone else's situation, we seem to "try on" someone else's shoes for a moment. But if an ad is cleverly made it will not just make us empathize it will also stir strong emotions in us. Strong enough to react impulsively and long enough to solve the insinuated issue with a purchase of the advertised product.

As Judith Williams (1978, p.70) once pointed out:

> This – a Lifestyle Kit – is precisely what ads offer us. In buying products with certain 'images' we create ourselves, our personality, our qualities, even our past and future. [...] We are both product and consumer; we consume, buy the product, yet we *are* the product. Thus our lives become our own creations, through buying; an identikit of different images of ourselves, created by different products.

And this patched-together, carefully created self often has a very unhealthy relationship with the ads we see.

So how unhealthy can advertising be for us?

Since advertising warps our self-perception and causes damaging insecurities, it can be lastingly unhealthy. Specifically fashion advertising is especially skilled at warping the self-perception because fashion is about being tall, beautiful, stylish, young, desirable, with a perfect and flawless body, dressed ideally for every situation and being socially a winner whilst having an extraordinarily lavish lifestyle. At this point, I would like to ask the reader to reflect and count how many people (and not any social media stars) he or she knows who fit this description. And now please think about how many fashion ads and influencer posts you remember which fit this description. Even if you work in the top notch of the modelling industry, you will still see more idealistic and retouched ads than real people.

When you look through a fashion or lifestyle magazine the advertising overshadows any editorial content (Winship, 1987). On average, a "September Issue" by the American *Vogue* will feature two thirds of advertising and the last third will be split between their own photography and a bit of actual writing. Just get yourself a copy and count each full advertising page per issue and then count the editorial pages with actual text (not product description next to a model wearing the items).

In 2014, Fashionista.com reported the numbers of three different September Issues: 631 ad pages in *Vogue*, 485 in *InStyle*, 215 in *Glamour* and 232 in *Vanity Fair* (Mau, 2014).

Of course, it's a Catch 22, since magazines are financially dependent on advertisers and will make space for as many ads as possible unless they firmly believe in a different business model. *Tank Magazine* was reportedly very cautious about whose ads they show and how many of them, raising the price per issue.

However, it is not uncommon for advertisers to use their position of power and withhold advertising if they are waiting for confirmation of a favourable editorial piece or a negative piece on a competitor (Lane, 2008).

"What is significant is that visual imagery, in colour especially, overshadows the written word. It has an immediate and rich impact the latter cannot inspire, while the associations of these colour images tend to stamp the firmest trace on magazine and reader's memory alike" Winship (1987, p. 55). The way we are used to consuming fashion, as this passage from the 1980s shows, is solely through visual representations of a make-believe world with make-believe people.

Erving Goffman (1976), one of the most influential sociologists of the twentieth century would call it "Commercial Realism" when advertisers try to present the advertising world in ways which could be real. He compares the staging of reality in advertising to that of staging a play: The viewer engages in acknowledging a make-believe world, the simulation of reality, of how things could be.

> The standard transformation employed in contemporary ads, in which the scene is conceivable in all detail as one that could in theory have occurred as pictured, providing us with a simulated slice of life; but although the advertiser does not seem intent on passing the picture off as a caught one, the understanding seems to be that we will not press him too far to account for just what sort of reality the scene has.
>
> (Goffman, 1976, p.15)

Knowing this, ads should appear strange to us, but most of the time they do not.

Warped self-perception and psychological implications of ads

Predominantly in fashion and beauty ads, an unrealistic standard of beauty is exaggerated and becomes this very commercial reality when perfect women are depicted – already thin and beautiful to begin with – and touched up in Photoshop during post-production.

What message do women, men and children receive when they see such imagery everywhere, from fashion magazines, to videos, to posters for social media campaigns? Anthony Cortese (1997) claims that women start feeling dissatisfied with their bodies, lose self-esteem and can even develop psychological problems such as eating disorders – all because of the unrealistic body image that one is asked to aspire to.

It is in fact almost impossible to live up to the beauty standards just as it is impossible to naturally have Barbie's body proportions. However, the secret desire to be model-perfect still permeates our society and darkens the psychological and physical (as well as financial) health of many women, men, young girls and boys who grow up with self-hatred – a very serious topic which Jean Kilbourne uncovered as early as 1979 when she made the documentary film "Killing us Softly". (The documentary has now been updated and currently has a fourth version).

One activist group called Adbusters has made it their mission to subvert advertising messages, point out their dangerous "side-effects" and raise the public's awareness. Because Adbusters uses the same codes and visual language in their subverted fashion ads, one can easily decode it and understand the social implications at a glance. For example, a series of spoof ads takes inspiration from Calvin Klein advertisements for the fragrance "Obsession", yet it depicts very different scenarios, such as a woman who is being sick above a toilet, already thin. The question arises whether she can ever be thin enough? Can she ever be happy with who she is? Is she perhaps similar to many other women?

The female body and its stereotypical thinness is presented to children at a very young age through dolls of unrealistic proportions. As the women grow up, they are groomed by brands to become consumers fuelled by a myriad of self-doubts that they mistakenly try to resolve through consumption. Figure 9.1 depicts a critical take on this issue by asking whether the female consumer is in fact voluntarily and freely consuming or is a victim and consumed by modern marketing, advertising and brands.

Gender and the objectification of bodies in advertising

Men and women are targeted in a different way which becomes evident when comparing ads in men's and women's fashion or lifestyle magazines. Have the traditional roles of men and women changed over the last decades and can we see this evidence in advertising?

It is true that especially women have been objectified in advertising for several decades now and are shown to be bodies without power, submissive to men and without a voice (Cortese, 1999). Oftentimes their bodies are "chopped up" only showing parts such as their breasts, stomachs, behinds and legs. What's worse is that through these images of subjugation it is made clear to men that the women are weak, there to be dominated by men, be it through sexual or violent actions (Kilbourne, 1979).

This becomes even more interesting if you consider that women in the entire US never fully attained equal rights since the Equal Rights Amendment

Figure 9.1 Is the female consumer happily consuming or is she being happily consumed? Author's original photography.

wasn't ratified (Kilbourne, 2019) despite attempts to do so in 1972. Far away in Europe, Germany saw equal rights for women only in 1977. So the dominating male was in fact a western cultural norm and continues to thrive in our visual culture.

One ad that is representative of objectification of women is the Weyenberg ad for Massagic Shoes from 1974. It shows a naked woman lying belly down on the floor, admiring a man's shoe. Her body is "chopped" as only her upper torso is shown and cut off from below her chest. She is happily smiling at the shoe, her eyes focused on the object and not the camera and the copy reads: "Keep her where she belongs..." This was in the 1970s, but have ads changed since then? Look at any ad by Sky Vodka for example, and you will see similar imagery.

Regarding "The Lag Between Advertising and Feminism" the *Atlantic* wrote in 2015:

And many ads today—be they for underwear or footwear or baby-powder-scented body spray—are in their way as retrograde as these specimens from the '70s. They can assume that women's consumer decisions are based on conceptions of male desire. They can assume that the key decision-maker in a commercial transaction, regardless of who spends the money, is a man.

We may well have come, in the words of Virginia Slims ads, "a long way, baby. But we still have far—very far—to go" (Garber, 2015).

Sexualization of children

Another aspect which needs to be looked at is the early sexualization of children and teens, which is now dominant in advertising.

According to Anthony Cortese (1999), women and men, as well as girls and boys, learn through advertising how they are expected to behave and what role they must play in society.

There are clear dangers in this advertising practice. An example is the viral video star Brendan Jordan, a 15-year-old self-proclaimed trans-gender boy who has been snapped up by American Apparel and extensively used in their campaign, highlighting his pre-teen sexual orientation. American Apparel's ads were highly criticized by advertising watchdogs during the reign of CEO and founder Dov Charney. He used underage girls, put them in sexually suggestive positions and photographed them himself. Some of these girls and some employees sued AA for molestation. Charney's ad campaigns were banned in some countries by advertising watchdogs due to indecency. The campaign with Brendan Jordan was conceived after Charney was made to leave the company, under the supervision of CEO Paula Schneider. Schneider reportedly wanted to tone down the overtly sexualized imagery of the brand, but insisted that she wanted to stay true to the original image by keeping it sexy and edgy. Brendan Jordan was a boy whom the brand gave a voice to, being able to come out of the closet through the campaign, she said in an interview with the *Independent* (Akbeiran, 2015).

The problem here is not the sexual orientation or activity of teenagers but rather the ethical implication. Is it ethically viable to exploit their sexuality for the purpose of fashion advertising? They are not allowed to buy alcohol in some countries but yet a fashion company is allowed to use them in a very vulnerable way and expose their sexuality to the rest of the world, in exchange for sales and profit increase.

These examples clearly show that advertising does not simply reflect changes in society but has its own influence on it. Because ads sell a dream and an enhanced or sometimes warped reality, gender is constructed within this "Commercial Reality" developing its very own meaning which in turn influences society. And as soon as the imagery in advertising becomes visible to a large number of people it can create a reaction and shape roles. If the imagery is viewed by consenting adults, they could arguably make an informed decision about the content, but when the most vulnerable members of society see them, namely children and teens, great harm can be done. Studies by psychologists and psychiatrists have shown negative impact on sexual behaviour, aggression, eating disorders in children and adolescents because they imitate (consciously and unconsciously) the role models presented to them, inhibiting their own healthy development. They engage in sexual actions and orientations before they are psychologically and emotionally ready which can leave them in an unhealthy state for the rest of their lives (Villani, 2001).

Case example: shock advertising and the Benetton case

Shock advertising is advertising that "deliberately, rather than inadvertently, startles and offends its audience by violating norms for social values and personal ideals". It relies on so-called shock tactics to get a message across by using offensive and graphic imagery – sometimes in combination with copy – all serving to put the recipients in a state of disturbed shock, fear or repulsion, gaining immediate attention. Oftentimes the imagery is full of cultural, religious, political or sexual taboos, loudly showing the sort of things that nobody wants to hear or see – yet it is inescapable due to being placed in the public sphere.

The origin of the terminology "shock advertising" is often attributed to the late 1980s and early 1990s due to Benetton's shocking fashion advertising imagery. The ads were criticized in many countries and in Germany had to go through court which then decided that it is indeed possible to use shock advertising in public. The photographer Oliviero Toscani was the mastermind behind the ads and his unique philosophy shaped the imagery. He showed a duck drenched in oil to make a point about human pollution of nature and the suffering of innocent animals; he showed David Kriby with AIDS on his death bed; he showed child labour in a third-world country; he showed the blood-stained uniform of a fallen soldier from ex-Yugoslavia; he showed a new-born baby covered in all the natural vernix and blood, with the umbilical cord still attached; he played with race, colour and ethnicities.

The images were criticized for manipulating people's emotions deliberately, for exploiting human (and animal) misery for purely financial gain and for being indecent. However, for instance in Germany, the ads were permitted on the grounds of the freedom of expression and the freedom of the press. From then on shock advertising was deemed permissible, as long as it does not offend human dignity (the depicted person is not ridiculed, mocked or humiliated).

As shock advertising became fashionable and legal, other companies followed suit, most notably Diesel, Calvin Klein, FCUK, the Body Shop but also charities, non-profit organizations and human-rights activists in order to raise awareness.

One example of a highly controversial print advertisement is Barnardo's "Child poverty campaign" (2003) advertisement which was banned by The Advertising Standards Authority after receiving 330 complaints. The ad showed a little baby with a seemingly live and large cockroach crawling out of its mouth "which is seen as a metaphorical reference to the destitution of many children" (Noel, 2010).

Bernardo's apologized about the campaign. "If you were personally distressed or offended by the images then we apologized. Having said that, we feel it is our duty to ensure the issue of child poverty in this country is no longer neglected and that is the reason we have run such a hard-hitting campaign" (Cozens, 2003).

The question here (and in most advertisements) is a purely ethical one: Is it worth disgusting the public with "hard-hitting" images to get attention, even if it is for a good cause? Is the good cause worth the harm its imagery causes in society? And could attention be obtained in a more responsible way?

Ill bodies and minds

Can fashion shock advertising support a good cause, too?

Fashion together has created a monster of self-doubt, a warped self-perception, eating disorders such as anorexia or bulimia and a myriad of psychological issues. With the help of Oliviero Toscani, a fashion campaign tried to provide an antidote to the harm that it has caused.

Toscani is an artist and believes that taboos should be broken, whether it is in art or in a fashion magazine. He wants to provoke people and test where the limits are. In an interview he recalled his collaboration with Benetton, stating that most managers and decision-makers were offended or embarrassed but ultimately granted him freedom as an artist. Regarding anorexia, he said:

> I'm interested in anorexia. It's about wanting to disappear, to become invisible, not wanting to be dependent. There are so many interesting implications in that illness. Initially, I did a short film on anorexia and,

later on, I started to do portraits with anorexic people. At a certain point a clothing company contacted me.

Toscani shot a campaign in collaboration with the fashion brand Nolita, using Isabelle Caro, a sickly anorexic model, in order to raise awareness about the illness. The model made it her life's mission to raise awareness about her illness which caused her to pass on at a very young age. In the campaign she was depicted nude with the words "No Anorexia" and the brand's logo. But when they put up billboards in Rome and Milan it caused an outrage and the Institute for Advertising Self-regulation (IAP) banned the campaign.

His work stands in contrast to the law suits which were filed against fast food chains that have led to obesity in children and adults due to their high-fat, highly-processed and high-calorie menus, the dangers of which had been down-played or omitted in ads. But both extremes of eating-related health issues are powered by advertising, be it through fashionable images of size zero models or all-you-can-eat menus.

Interview with Jean Kilbourne

Figure 9.2 Jean Kilbourne.

Jean Kilbourne is internationally recognized for her ground-breaking work on the image of women in advertising and for her critical studies of alcohol and tobacco advertising. In the late 1960s she began her exploration of the connection between advertising and several public health issues, including violence against women, eating disorders, and addiction, and launched a movement to promote media literacy as a way to prevent these problems. A radical and original idea at the time, this approach is now mainstream and an integral part of most prevention programs.

Q: Fashion advertising and media communication in general shows perfection: Beautiful models, beautiful clothes, beautiful settings – a dream landscape. It includes women, men and children. How do you perceive the dream which is pushed on us by the fashion and advertising industry?

JK: There is research that it is harmful, that it affects self esteem. It's particularly damaging to women because, although men are objectified more than they used to be, there still isn't that kind of pressure on men to look a certain way, whereas for women there is. The advent of Photoshop has changed everything as has the Internet because now women and girls do this to ourselves. We put images out there, so the pressure is even more intense and more damaging, I would argue, than even in the past.

Many people feel that advertising is trivial and that therefore it doesn't really matter. My argument has always been that it is not trivial, that it affects us in fact very deeply and, in many ways, very negatively. I was the first one to speak about this way back in the late 1960s. I made the film "Killing Us Softly: Advertising's Image of Women" in 1979. Since then I have remade the movie three times, with the latest version being in 2010. I have been updating it all along and it is very widely used all around the world.

Q: You have probably seen the most recent fashion imagery that shows imperfection. Fashion brands are using models who have a variety of body types, might have disabilities, pigmentation deviations etc. Brands are selling it under the flag of being socially inclusive. Do you think fashion advertising has to demonstrate social exclusion in order to remain aspirational?

JK: Two things: I think it is very important for ads to show a wide range of body types of women, because at the moment there basically is still only one body type considered desirable. Even the "plus-size" models are still thinner than the average American woman. I think showing a wide range of bodies and colours is important and would make a difference.

I also think that most advertisers, of course, are doing this for public relations. They're doing this to demonstrate to their consumers that they are hip and open-minded, so I don't think necessarily that they are doing this out of the goodness of their hearts.

But I don't care because what's important is that we see a wide range of what's considered beautiful because up until now we've just had this one definition and it excludes most women and really does have an effect on how women and girls feel about ourselves. I think that it is the push to have advertising be more diverse, more inclusive, more representative of real people that is good.

It seems to me that people in the fashion industry would be interested in working with a variety of body types rather than to be stuck with such limited images. It is also an exciting opportunity for students to have a broader palette to work with.

Q: A really important topic: Children. Advertising has been for a long time and still are using children. They are sexualizing them, showing them in inappropriate settings. What is your take on using children in fashion campaigns, such as the controversial one by American Apparel who used Brendan Jordan, a self-proclaimed trans-gender child (15 years old at the time of the campaign), in their campaign? What should the future advertisers industry think about sexualizing children? What is your view on this?

JK: I talked about the sexualization of children in the original version of "Killing Us Softly" back in 1979 and I wrote a book about it called *So Sexy So Soon*. So I think this is a very big problem. For the most part I am not in favour of legislation and that sort of thing, but I think there should be tremendous pressure on advertisers not to do this, not to sexualize children, and there could be legal guidelines. But mostly change will happen because of public pressure, through consumers protesting. Of course, this doesn't happen until enough people realize that this is a very bad thing to be doing.

People have to see it, take it seriously and realize that this is damaging to children. And the research is very clear that this is indeed damaging to children. On my website there is a resource list that includes an American Psychological Association report on sexualization of girls in advertising and the harm that it does. Different countries have different regulations. In the United States it is extremely difficult to put any limitations on advertising due to free speech and treating corporations like people etc. but in other countries it is more possible.

I think this is one of the most serious issues in advertisng. What happens when children are sexualized? For one thing sexualizing children is normalized, which encourages paedophilia and also encourages people to blame the victim. A few years ago a little girl was sexually assaulted and a judge here in the United States said that she was seductive. She was five years old. Sexualizing children also damages children because it encourages them to think of themselves as objects, which does an enormous amount of harm.

This issue is one of the most serious in fashion advertising. There needs to be a multi-pronged approach, including consumer education, guidelines insofar as they are possible, some legislation and, in general, many people saying, "This is not okay, this has got to stop".

Q: Let's talk about "Shock advertising", which first entered the fashion scene with Oliviero Toscani's controversial campaigns for Benetton. On the one hand he was really ahead of his time in terms of inclusivity – black and white and Asian models – he put everyone together. But at the same time he was using very sensitive imagery, shocking things to sell multi-coloured sweaters.

JK: And that is the problem really. The problem is not the images themselves, as they are often images we probably should see and should be aware of, but it is when they are attached to buying stuff. What does this have to do with each other, a dying AIDS patient with – like you said – multi-coloured sweaters? This to me just trivializes the whole issue and exploits our emotions in order to sell us something. It's not the images – it's the use of them in the service of selling us stuff that is the problem. If these images were used to sell donations to charities or something like that, that would be a different thing, but this is trivializing, it's exploitive and ultimately it also can desensitize us to these issues. If we are surrounded by these images being used to sell us something, we can get used to them and they cease to shock and that becomes a problem.

Have you heard of the expression "compassion fatigue"? It's what happens as people are overwhelmed by images and then feel numb about them. It can happen not just with advertising but in general. When we harden our hearts to these realities, it is dangerous to our society.

Q: The visual communication of fashion advertising often shows weird, strange and bizarre images of women and sometimes men, with violence (like the highly sexual and controversial D&G ad from 2007, with four men standing over a woman on the ground) or chopped up body parts. What do you think about ads where women are reduced to a few chopped up body parts in ads, with no face, no voice and no power, withdrawn?

JK: Often these images are violent and that, of course, is a big problem. Using violent images like this, especially when violence is eroticized and made sexy, does a huge amount of harm. It normalizes violence against women and it perpetuates stereotypes and it also makes it more likely that people will blame the victim.

Q: My last question is about the future of the fashion marketing professionals. They will be selling fashion, they might be creating ad campaigns, they will be in marketing and working with brands. Is there any message that you would like to convey to them? How can they make sure that they are doing their job, perhaps under pressure to meet certain business targets, but at the same time, students think about ethical issues, they want to ensure their ethical integrity and want to have a clear conscience. What would you recommend to them?

JK: One thing that I recommend is that they find allies, that they find other people who share their wish to be ethical, because it's difficult to do this alone. This is why the 3% Project has been so important – because women and men in advertising agencies got together and said, "We don't want to do this anymore". So that is one thing. Also, having allies and being in groups like this can help refine one's own opinions.

Secondly, these issues should be brought up in fashion schools, in business schools and there should be a strong ethical component in all schools where these questions are raised. I've often told my audiences: "Ask yourself these questions before you have a mortgage. Think about what you want to do before you are locked into a job where you can't afford to rock the boat". So raise these issues early on.

Back in the day when advertisers, or at least the ones with power, were almost entirely male, I would say things like "Put your mother's face, your daughter's face, your sister's face, your wife's face into this ad. How do you feel about that?" Now there are more women with power in the field (although still not enough!) but it is still important to ask oneself, "How would you feel if this was *your* daughter, *your* son?" Make it human, make it real and make it personal.

When I've addressed advertising audiences, I have often said, if the only way you can sell the product is to exploit and diminish people, what does that say about your product? It's important to think about what it is exactly that you are selling. In fashion, one thing that could happen that would be very good is not just a bigger range of models but a bigger range of fashion for different body types. Because at the moment fashion is designed for women who are very tall and thin and narrow. Let's redesign fashion to make all women and men feel more attractive. This opens the door to more creative possibilities for the fashion industry and for students.

Regulatory bodies

Advertising has come a long way since its early days, both in terms of regulations that are limiting it and social norms which it has pushed away. It is important to understand that brands and the forceful advertising industry do not have complete control over the messages which they spread. Individuals have the right to complain and there are many reasons why the authorities might take a complaint seriously and recall an ad. Advertising is viewed by different people, including children and those people come from various ethnicities and religions with a wide variation of sensitivity or tolerance towards advertising content. For the benefit of society, not everything can be shown openly.

Reasons why ads are recalled are often inappropriate content, sexualization of children, degradation of women, sexism and racism, indecency, lies or false advertising. In the fashion industry, the latter often occurs when women are excessively photo shopped in order to promote a beauty product.

Who steps in and what can be done?

First and foremost, there are laws which prohibit unlawful and illegal advertising.

However, many ads can pass legal constraints but are nevertheless harmful to society, so in this case advertising watchdogs step in.

For instance, in Europe the European Advertising Standards Alliance (EASA) is the coordination point for the views of national advertising self-regulatory organizations throughout Europe.

Under its umbrella, there are regulatory bodies for each country:

Austria – Österreichischer Werberat
Belgium – Jury d'Ethique Publicitaire
Czech Republic – Rada Pro Reklamu – RPR
Denmark – ReklameForum
Finland – Liiketapalautakunta – LTL
France – Bureau de Vérification de la Publicité – BVP
Germany – Deutscher Werberat – DW
Germany – Zentrale zur Bekämpfung unlauteren Wettbewerbs
Greece – Enossi Diafimistikon Etairion Ellados – EDEE
Hungary – Önszabályozó Reklám Testület
Ireland – Advertising Standards Authority for Ireland – ASAI
Italy – Insituto dell'Autodisciplina Pubblicitaria – IAP
Lithuania – Lithuanian Advertising Bureau
Netherlands – Stichting Reclame Code – SRC
Poland – Rada Reklamy (RR)
Portugal – Instituto Civil da Autodisciplina da Publicidade – ICAP
Slovakia – Rada Pre Reklamu – RPR
Slovenia – Slovenska Oglasevalska Zbornica – SOZ
Switzerland – Commission Suisse pour la Loyauté / Schweizerische
    Lauterkeitskommission – CSL/SLK
United Kingdom (UK) – Advertising Standards Authority – ASA

The ASA in the UK for example, take action to protect consumers when complaints are made by businesses and individuals to ban ads which are misleading, harmful, offensive or irresponsible.

In 2017 alone, the ASA resolved over 29,000 complaints relating to just under 16,000 ads and a further 5,425 cases on their own initiative with a total of 4,584 ads being either changed or removed (ASA, 2018).

Sensory overload: ads are all-present

Rarely fashion brands choose to opt out of advertising. Zara, the top fast fashion retailer reportedly only spends 3 per cent of its revenue on advertising. So how can Zara remain successful without the ads? The retailer has a completely different strategy which builds on artificial limitation of goods, prime retail locations and beautiful interiors. Since Zara copies luxury fashion brands which amply advertise, one can assume that Zara then reaps the benefits by selling the cheap knock-off versions of the original garments at a fraction of the price. However, consumers will not feel bombarded by advertising coming from Zara, as one would from many other brands which surround us with an unhealthy amount of information, attacking our senses.

Raimund (2008) notes that the 10 Commandments only contain 279 words. Castro and Lewis (2011) add that Lincoln's Gettysburg Address contains only 266 words. Yet on a daily basis we are bombarded with thousands of advertising messages everywhere in public and equally in our private lives. Not only does this give room for psychological harm which was discussed in this chapter, it also can have a direct negative effect on our well-being through the sheer volume of unnecessary information. Sensory overload is a term which is now well known and used by psychologists and doctors as a condition which leads to negative physical as well as psychological states such as an increased heart rate, blood pressure and breathing, anxiety, confusion, a feeling of distress, aggression, sadness, agitation or erratic behaviour to the point of mental breakdowns, neurological problems and even seizures (in people with predispositions such as autism these occurrences are even more likely to happen). In terms of marketing, when brands compete with each other to attract and reach the customer, they are either causing sensory harm through overload or even worse, the consumer becomes indifferent to the multitude of messages, which is a psychological way of protecting oneself, rendering the marketing messages ineffective to a certain degree.

The question arises whether this bombardment by marketing and advertising signals is something we should accept or something we should amend. What would the streets of a city look like if suddenly there was no advertising? How do people find out about products or trends? There are a few places which choose to amend the amount of sensory stimulation for the benefit of the people or due to political ideology.

Case example: ad-free places – Grenoble, São Paulo and North Korea

In some cases, governments and the mayors of cities step in to regulate advertising:

Grenoble and São Paulo have recently banned outdoor advertising for the benefit of its population and there have already been positive reactions by both inhabitants of the cities and business owners.

Figure 9.3 São Paulo, Brazil, by night without any billboards or notable ads, 2016. Image source: Pixabay by Zabarov.

São Paulo: A city of more than 11 million inhabitants and each one can walk down the streets without the bombardment by advertising messages. In 2006, São Paulo's populist mayor, Gilberto Kassab, passed the so-called "Clean City Law", outlawing the use of all outdoor advertisements, including on billboards, transit, and in front of stores. A total of 15,000 outdoor ad spaces were taken down.

This was not done without some hesitation as local businesses and citizens feared that the ban would cause revenue loss of $133 million and 20,000 job losses. However, since then the city has been thriving with 70 per cent of city dwellers being in favour of the ban (Cutis, 2011).

Grenoble:

Eric Piolle, the mayor of the French city of Grenoble since 2014, is not only dreaming of a green and sustainable city of the future, he has also taken action against visual pollution. The city chose not to renew its advertising contract with giant JCDecaux instead removing 326 billboards. (Dejean, 2014)

North Korea is an almost "ad-free" environment due to communist politics. The only types of advertising which are allowed are political propaganda.

Figure 9.4 Grenoble, France. A city that banned most outdoor advertising. Image source: Pixabay.

Architect Philipp Meuser edited the first-ever architectural guide on Pyongyang in 2011. He shares his views on the ad-free streets.

In those countries which are underpinned by a Communist system, architecture and urban planning can be experienced in unadulterated form – there are no advertising signs nor garish, neon-lit billboards. We are seeing design and construction carried out under laboratory conditions. No matter how fascinating such an untarnished city may be from the architectural standpoint, its very nakedness reveals a state which could scarcely be more totalitarian. Where there is no advertising there is no competition either. Billboards are replaced by propaganda posters which have been hand-painted and indeed call for considerable artistic expertise. Although very nice to look at, their content is anything but amusing, eg 'Our ideology, our fighting spirit, our way of life – let everything be as our forefathers decreed!', or 'A strong country – let us restore the glorious past of our forefathers!' These are calls-to-arms which in other countries would be attributed to radical political parties. And yet, because the streets are so densely hung with such morale-boosting slogans – in a similar manner to advertising signage in the West – we can only surmise and indeed hope that they scarcely register with the people fleetingly rushing past them.

(Meuser, 2016)

Figure 9.5 Pyongyang, North Korea. The sign reads: "white words: ideology / fight sprit / life style; blue words: all about above, we will follow Kim Jeongeun". Image credit: © Philipp Meuser. Image kindly provided by Philipp Meuser of DOM-Publishers, from their book "Pyongyang. Architectural and Cultural Guide", 2012.

Is there really no advertising in North Korea? According to the BBC (2016), "for the past decade or so the only evidence of advertising in Pyongyang had been the handful of billboards for Pyonghwa Motors, which borrow popular slogans from state propaganda campaigns" (Abrahamian, 2016).

But the country seems to be slowly awakening to the new discipline of consumerism which they understand as propaganda for consumer products.

Interview with Evgeniya Sabelnikova

Figure 9.6 Photo of Russian actress Evgeniya Sabelnikova in the 1970s.

Evgeniya Sablenikova (Евгения Сабельникова) was a famous Russian movie star in the 1970s and 1980s at the country's largest film studios, including Mosfilm, starring in more than 23 films and being the voice actress for many more. She was also a model at the Dom Modeley, the most famous fashion house of the former USSR.

Q: In the USSR, a country under communist rule, how was political propaganda perceived by the people?

ES: It was either not noticed at all or if it was, then perceived with light and habitual repulsion. If it was written stupidly, people would laugh on the inside, but it was uncommon to do it publicly. The communist propaganda was like a restaurant which always serves bad food without fail. But in the 1970s, when the regime was not as strict as it was under Stalin, young people began to mock it verbally.

Q: Was there any advertising for consumer products?

ES: None on TV, none on the radio, none in the printed media. Zero in journals. There were very rare billboard ads: "Fly Aeroflot!" a poster would proclaim. But when Aeroflot is the only state airline in the entire country, what else would you fly with? And people used to joke about such ads. There were a few advertisements for holidays in Crimea or Sochi, sort of emulating other countries, but again, where else were people going to go on holiday but there?

But there was a magazine called *Rabotnica* ["Работница",] a journal for the interests of working women, founded in 1914] which had editorials with illustrations and photos of what to wear and what was fashionable at the moment. It also reported about the Soviet factories which were sewing the clothes, but everyone knew that they were awful!

Q: Apart from the journal, how did people know what is fashionable?

ES: There were three or four unofficial and unmentionable methods to find out.

First there were political TV shows – in the style of a documentary – reporting on the terrible life of people in capitalist countries with much critique and a political agenda. They showed thriving capitalist countries such as France, England, the USA and there were 3 to 5 minute sequences showing the poor people who were suffering from capitalism, such as the unemployed on the streets of New York etc. and everyone, especially women, watched the show. "Look at this jacket that unemployed guy is wearing on the street in New York! That is a nice jacket!" someone would exclaim. Or: "There, the women in the background in Paris – see the dress, see the cut? We can make this". Women watched the shows to find out what's in fashion and then they would copy the styles and sew them at home.

Then one day, suddenly the journal *Burda* was available in a very limited number of copies. It was worth gold! If you had this magazine you were a queen! Not only did you get the images of what was in fashion but also the patterns to sew. And we had wonderful fabrics in stores, in abundance and not expensive. So women bought the fabrics and sewed themselves. This *Burda* became very popular.

Another method was through friends, those rare people who got to go abroad and brought back mail-order catalogues. The catalogues were either resold for a very high price or kept at home where friends could come to visit and flip through the magazine the whole day long if they wished. There was not just fashion but interiors, too.

Q: You worked as a model in the famous Moscow Fashion House, the "Dom Modeley" [Общесоюзный дом моделей одежды (ОДМО)] – can you tell a bit more about it?

ES: Yes, these were the centers of the USSR's fashion, in St. Petersburg and Moscow only. It was Russia's way of competing with global fashion, of having something similar to the catwalk shows abroad, to show that we were as creative and prosperous as the capitalist countries.

Often foreigners would be invited to the catwalk presentations to see how beautiful our women were and how well they were dressed. Like in the West, normal people could not get in to see the shows.

Figure 9.7 From the personal archive of Evgeniya Sabelnikova: High-school ball in the 1960s – group photo, St Petersburg, Russia. The clothing would have been either purchased in stores or hand-made following the latest fashion trends, such as those found in the national magazine *Rabotnica*, which also supplied fashion patterns.

Figure 9.8 From the personal archive of Evgeniya Sabelnikova: High-school ball in the 1960s – individual photo, St Petersburg, Russia.

Other attendants were the political elite and the top elite from show business like actors, singers etc. They were allowed to come and watch the shows but needed a special permit to order clothes. The clothes were great designs by very talented designers like Slava Zaitsev, who was the top couturier in the 1970s and is now world famous. But the communist party members were not allowed to purchase the clothes and had to come in the typical suits that were appropriate for political figures.

Further reading

Blasberg, D. (2014) Harper's Bazaar, Marc and Sofia: The Dreamy Team. Available at: www.harpersbazaar.com/fashion/designers/a3169/marc-jacobs-sofia-coppola-0914/

Carter, C. and Steiner, L. (2004) *Critical Readings: Media and Gender*. Maidenhead: Open University Press (McGraw-Hill Education).

Chomsky, N. (1998) *Profit over People: Neoliberalism and the Global Order*. New York: Seven Stories Press.

Cortese, A. J. (1999) *Provocateur: Images of Women and Minorities in Advertising*. Boston: Rowman & Littlefield.

Cull, N. J., Holbrook Culbert, D. and Welch, D. (2003) *Propaganda and Mass Persuasion: A Historical Encyclopedia, 1500 to the Present*. Santa Barbara: ABC-Clio Inc.

Ellis, N., Fitchett, J., Higgins, M., Jack, G., Lim, M., Saren, M. and Tadajewski, M. (2011) *Marketing: A Critical Textbook*. London: Sage Publications.

Goffman, E. (1976) *Gender Advertisements*. New York: Harper Torchbooks.

Hlynsky, D. and Langford, M. (2015) *Window-Shopping through the Iron Curtain*. London: Thames & Hudson.

Kelso, T. (2018) *The Social Impact of Advertising: Confessions of an (Ex-)Advertising Man*. Lanham, MD: Rowman & Littlefield Publishers.

Kilbourne, J. (1999) *Can't Buy ME Love: How Advertising Changes the Way We Think and Feel*. New York: Touchstone.

Klein, N. (2010) *No Logo*. 10th anniversary edn. London: Fourth Estate.

Levine, D. L. and Kilbourne, J. (2009) *So Sexy So Soon*. New York: Ballantine Books Inc.

Meuser, P. (ed.) (2012) *Architectural and Cultural Guide Pyongyang*. Berlin: DOM Publishers.

Miles, S. (1998) *Consumerism: As a Way of Life*. Thousand Oaks, CA: SAGE Publications.

Sheehan, K. (2013) *Controversies in Contemporary Advertising*. 2nd edn. Thousand Oaks, CA: SAGE Publications.

Taflinger, R. F. (2011) *Advantage: Consumer Psychology and Advertising*. 1st edn. Dubuque, IA: Kendall Hunt.

The United Nations of Photography. In Coversation: Oliviero Toscani. Available at: https://unitednationsofphotography.com/2016/01/25/in-conversation-oliviero-toscani/

Williamson, J. (1978) *Decoding Advertisements: Ideology and Meaning in Advertising*. London: Marion Boyars.

Winship, J. (1987) *Inside Womens's Magazines*. London: Pandora.

The future of fashion marketing

10

Trends and opportunities

Chapter topics

The Fashion Carousel

The 'Fashion Carousel' is a figurative representation of the cyclical nature of the fashion system which is ever changing whilst it rotates and recycles ideas from the past.

The Carousel consists of elements such as textiles, design, production, retail, marketing, media and technology, further elements are culture and history, politics and economics. In every era, certain trends were prominent and we recognize them when looking back at history, revisiting many of them in modern times. For example, fashion pieces such as shoulder pads saw different uses (and materials) in the last 2000 plus years:

Figure 10.1 The Fashion Carousel. Author's original illustration.

They were part of a Roman Centurion's dress, later appearing in medieval armour suits for men, European military coats at the end of the seventeenth century featured external shoulder pads called epaulettes. In the late 1800s American football players received shoulder padding as protection from injury. In the 1930s they were introduced ino womenswear and later in the 1980s became the silhouette of the power suit for women. Yet again in 2009, Olivier Rousteing presented a collection for Balmain which emphasized the shoulders. Most likely, we will see the shoulder pads in fashion over and over again.

Mini skirts are another interesting type of clothing, which, throughout history, transferred from men to women, making itself prominent in the twentieth century, so much so that a "Hemline Index" was created, establishing a connection between the fluctuating length of a hemline and political, economic and social events.

Heels were worn by women and men alike in the last centuries, representing status and wealth, social position and style. Now mostly attributed to womenswear, the shape and size of a heel will change with seasons and shoemakers.

The tight-fitting sheath dress of ancient Egypt, adorned with jewels, precious stones and metals, became highly fashionable in the 1920s when the tomb of Tutankhamun was discovered and has inspired a collection by Karl Lagerfeld for Chanel in the twenty-first century.

Figure 10.2 Russian economist Nikolai Kondratiev lived from 1892–1932 and invented the 'Kondratiev Waves'. Author's original illustration.

Because fashion picks up on, interprets and expresses various events in society, politics, economy, technology, and even law (just think of sumptuary laws), there is a correlation between trends and economic business cycles.

There are various theories on the cyclical nature of economic trends and the length of a cycle, ranging from a few years to several decades. The following economists suggested waves and cycles of varying lengths: Kondratiev (54 years), Kuznets (18 years), Juglar (9 years), and Kitchin (about 4 years) and finally the Austrian economist Joseph Schumpeter, who later in his life became a professor at Harvard University, took all these theories and combined them into one, bringing the theory by Kondratiev to the attention of the western world.

The original "Kondratiev Waves" (sometimes called K-waves or Supercycles; sometimes spelled *Kondratieff*) is a theory invented by the Russian scientist Nikolai Kondratiev in the early twentieth century in Russia.

A Kondratiev Wave is a long-term economic cycle in a capitalist economy, believed to result from technological innovation and produce a long period of prosperity during the expansion phase, but at a certain point it halts during a stagnation phase and ultimately results in economic downturn during recession. This Cycle or Wave would last between four to six decades on average.

Although modern economists have opposing opinions on whether this theory is accurate and acceptable, the ones who acknowledge its validity recognize several such waves which are all connected to innovation and social change.

Table 10.1   Kondratiev Waves.

	Duration of Wave	Innovation
First Kondratiev Wave	1780 to 1830	Steam engine
Second Kondratiev Wave	1830 to to 1880	Steel and rail industries
Third Kondratiev Wave	1880 to 1930	Electricity and chemicals
Fourth Kondratiev Wave	1930 to 1970	Petrochemicals, mass production and automobiles
Fifth Kondratiev Wave	1970 to present	Information technology and telecommunications
Sixth Kondratiev Wave	Present to future	Medicine, health and biotech; post-information technology

Five distinct Kondratiev waves have been recognized since its invention with discussions pointing towards an imminent sixth one (Kenton, 2018).

If you return to Chapters 1 and 2, you can look at developments of the industrial revolution and the changes which the fashion industry experienced, comparing them to Kondratiev's Waves. The industrial revolution and consequent production of fashion goods runs in parallel with the first Kondratiev Wave. The innovation of railways and electricity helped to expand advertising and public relations, whilst petrochemicals and the automotive industries sped up and facilitated a global production and consumption of fashion en masse. Modern communication and consumption practices are connected to the fifth Kondratiev Wave with the rise of digital media and devices. Finally, present-day innovations of medicine and health as well as biotech include studies of neuroscience, AI and genes which are connected to the latest trends in the fashion industry, as illustrated in the latter part of this chapter.

What is trend forecasting?

Future fashion forecasts are now offered by specialist companies and can help businesses detect patterns and trends helping designers and marketers alike to position themselves competitively for the future.

Historically, this form of fashion forecasting can be traced to the industrial revolution (as explained in Chapter 1), which saw the clothing and the textiles trade expand and created the need to better predict and set upcoming colour and style trends.

In the beginning of the twentieth century, America was looking at France and its production of colours and textiles as a trend indicator but later its very own Textile Color Card Association of the USA (TCCA) was set up and told brands and stores which colours to produce and sell in order to meet popular customer demands.

By 1930 the TCCA played a major role in defining the colours and their names for all manner of fashion as well as government related items such as uniforms, ribbons, medals, and flags. Another 20 years later, the TCCA membership of subscribing business grew internationally. This expansion led to the creation of industry specific trends and colour books sponsored by those industries and direct consulting to individual companies (Holland and Jones, 2017).

In Europe, from the 1960s onwards, agencies such as Promostyl, Nelly Rodi and Li Edelkoort (Trend Union) emerged, offering colour, trend and visual forecast in colourful and often quirky books.

Further agencies followed, such as WGSN (Worth Global Style Network) in the late 1990s and Trendstop and Stylus after 2000. All these agencies operate internationally and have global offices around the world.

Textile fairs and exhibitions such as Premiere Vision, Pitti Filati and Techtextil also grew to become authorities on trends and now help the fashion industry to prepare for the upcoming seasons by giving insights into the raw material trends which are turned into clothes.

However, critics have pointed out that behemoth WGSN and its trend predictions are so influential, that they forecast and predict textile trends several years in advance, influencing textile manufacturers. This in theory means that any fashion brand is selecting materials which were dictated by WGSN (Seto, 2017).

WGSN is indeed a very powerful and strong influencer in trend reports and trend prediction. It was founded by brothers Julian and Marc Worth in London in 1998, growing explosively and changing owners to parent company Ascential in 2005. The service (like most of the modern trend forecasting agencies) looks at a broad variety of influences on the fashion industry, such as textiles, colour, fashion, catwalks, lifestyle, interiors, cosmetics, marketing, consumer behaviour, retail and innovation.

Trend forecasting today thus has to look at society, science, technology, politics and consumer behaviour alike because ultimately, fashion is a catalyst for all of these elements. Analysing the potential of these sometimes emerging and quiet developments or full blown hypes, there is a chance to make a strong indication for the future.

Trends to be aware of

Developments such as neuroscience and machine learning, emotions and curation, Gen Z & Gen Alpha, emerging markets and globalization, inclusivity and sustainability are arguably main trends that fashion brands should be aware of. As they are developing, it is equally important not to lag behind with an ethical approach to the use and application of those advances.

Table 10.2 Global trends fashion needs to be aware of.

Neuroscience and machine learning	Neuroscience is a modern science of the nervous system and brain, part of which aims to uncover how it works. Areas that this science might serve includes marketing, trying to tap into emotions, mood, memory and impulses of the human.
	Machine learning is a modern science which develops artificial intelligence (AI) and machines which can support, copy or even rival human intelligence by gathering and analysing data in order to make decisions. Areas that this science might serve includes marketing, retail and online advertising.
	Both have been steadily entering the world of marketing and some brands such as Zara, Rigby & Peller, Prada, Burberry and Ralph Lauren have introduced AI into their retail environments and merchandising practices as well as advertising. It is expected that more fashion businesses will integrate AI, changing the traditional way consumers interact with brands.
Emotions and curation	Neuroscience has revealed that humans are driven by emotions and many decisions are based on them rather than the rational parts of our brain. It is thus interesting for marketers to tap into the consumers' emotions to connect them to the brand and influence purchase decisions.
	One way of enhancing the emotional appeal is by offering a curated shopping experience.
	The definition of curation is "the selection and care of objects to be shown in a museum or to form part of a collection of art, an exhibition", as stated by the Cambridge Dictionary (2019) and it has been a common practice in museums but over the last decades it has been applied to marketing and retail as well as online environments.
	Offline, consumers enter department stores and flagship stores like a museum, experiencing a carefully selected display of objects, often interactive. Concepts stores such as 10 Corso Como, the now closed Colette or Dover Street Market achieved a fusion of cultural space, commerce and exhibition space, setting trends in what is "cool".
	Online websites are aiming to deliver the same experience. According to Elliot van Buskirk (2010), in online spaces consumers find themselves in curated environments such as Spotify which curates music, Facebook that curates the web or news websites which curate the news.
	The future will likely see further demand for curated ad emotional brand experiences.

(continued)

Table 10.2 (Cont.)

Generations Z and Alpha	Following the Millennials, Generation Z was born between 1995 and 2009 whilst the even younger Generation Alpha was born after 2010.
	Both are absolute digital natives (with current children sitting in their buggies playing on iPads), they are very interesting targets to marketers who are already researching those two demographic groups in order to understand how they can sell to them. These youngsters are a global and international as they were recently born in strong emerging markets.
	Brands are already trying to tap into and understand their future consumers who are transitioning from childhood to adulthood.
Inclusivity	According to the Cambridge Dictionary (2019), Inclusivity is "the quality of trying to include many different types of people and treat them all fairly and equally" and is a major trend in fashion. With brands embracing a wide scope of sizes and body shapes, ethnicities and genders the trend is steadily encompassing many industries including fashion which has a history of being highly excluding.
Emerging markets and globalization	Emerging economies such as Brazil, India, Russia, China (in short BRIC) are economies that are on their way to becoming developed countries. They have financial infrastructure, GDP growth, established industries or increasing industrialization, social stability and an overall high growth rate.
	They are a lucrative investment for established brands because those countries have a rising middle class with numerous customers who have relatively recently obtained more disposable income and are eager to buy into designer brands.
	The trend shows consumer demand and consumer spending across several age groups and demographics in new markets.
Sustainability	Sustainability famously means "meeting our own needs without compromising the ability of future generations to meet their own needs".
	In includes environmental, economic. social aspects and overall ethical aspects and should ideally create a world where ecological integrity is maintained, communities can thrive and human rights are respected (McGill, 2019).
	The sustainability trend means that consumers are keen to have sustainable products and buy guilt-free. Equally manufacturers and brands have to demonstrate that their practices are indeed sustainable.
	However, any ethical and sustainable practices that brands communicated are questionable with consumers understanding that facts could potentially be twisted, thus "Greenwashing" and making false claims.

Interview with Roger Tredre on trends

Roger Tredre, journalist, author and lecturer, is Course Leader in MA Fashion Communication at Central Saint Martin's, London. From 1999 to 2006, he was editor-in-chief of trend forecasting giant WGSN. In the 1990s, he was arts correspondent at *The Observer* and fashion correspondent at *The Independent*. He has also edited trends magazine *Viewpoint* and contributed to magazines and newspapers worldwide, ranging from *Vanity Fair* to *The International Herald Tribune, The Times, Vogue, Vanity Fair, GQ*. He is co-author of 'The Great Fashion Designers', published in 2009 by Berg.

1. Neuroscience and machine learning

The latest developments in neuroscience give opportunities to target customers more effectively, whilst artificial machine learning means we might adapt to a life alongside intelligent machines, humanoid robots or other life-imitating machines. In fashion, retail giants have been using machine-learning algorithms to forecast demand and set prices for years already. According to Amit Sharma (2016) retailers would be better off if they started thinking more like tech companies, using AI and machine learning not just to predict how to stock stores and staff shifts, but also to

Figure 10.3 Roger Tredre.

dynamically recommend products and set prices that appeal to individual consumers.

Q: How do you see the future of fashion in relation to these technological advances?

RT: The fashion industry has always wanted to understand consumers better, but the volatility and unpredictability of fashion still defy the best efforts of AI and machine learning. That said, these technologies used carefully can massively improve the likelihood of creating the right kind of clothes for the right kind of customers. AI has a role to play for mass market fashion, but it will never completely replace gut instinct and the chance element behind many trends, both micro and macro.

2. Emotions and curation

Emotionally charging brand comms means turning them into a powerful mechanism that can engage the viewer to such an extent that he or she feels compelled to share the ad within the social media channels, thus turning the comms into a viral sensation. But what does it mean if people voluntarily help a brand to spread its advertising?

Emotions also play a big part in the need for curated spaces: Concept stores or curated online selections, along with copy text, make shopping for fashion experiential and engaging. There is a need for spaces that let people unwind from a fast-paced lifestyle and these are ironically shops.

Q: There seems to be a contradictory trend of strong emotional involvement by consumers in the brands whilst at the same time they need to detox from them, ironically, often in the same space. What is your view on this?

RT: Talking about physical space first: if the brand can support the consumer in the process of unwinding or playing, then there is no need for a hard sell. When I pass by a Starbucks mid-morning, I know there is a strong likelihood that I will find a comfortable sofa to sit on and check my emails. The purchase of a cappuccino is not the key appeal for me. I go into Starbucks for a pleasant experience tinged with a low-key emotion. A retailer who provides more reasons to visit a store beyond the purchase of product inevitably widens the customer base. Through social media, brands can also widen their appeal by tapping into and supporting the values of their customers.

There is a calculated risk, of course, that consumers can become tired by every brand seeking to emotionally engage. It will be interesting to see how quickly Generation Z becomes cynical about all this!

3. Sustainability

The current "green" trend has been developing for some years now and has reached many consumers who want to shop guilt free, regardless of whether it is luxury, fast fashion or throwaway fashion. Brands can no longer ignore the dark side of fashion especially after the media continues to publish accusations of human rights violations or dangerous chemicals in the poorest countries of the world where tons of garments are made every day.

Whether it is fast fashion's H&M or a luxury brand like Gucci all are keen to certify that their supply chain meets the "SA8000" standards of the independent inspection group Bureau Veritas, the efforts by brands are evident.

Q: How do fashion brands cater to the ethical needs of consumers and how can they do this through communications? Do you see any dangers in "greenwashing" the consumers (i.e. pretending to be sustainable only to be then found out)?

RT: Consumers, in my view, are very aware of the likelihood of so-called greenwashing because there's been so much of it about. Fashion companies have to engage at a very senior executive level to work out how best to guarantee ethical sourcing and sustainable production. The momentum from consumers and consumer pressure groups has been building very slowly, to the frustration of many in the sustainable fashion movement, but the important point is that it is still building. The heightened awareness globally about plastic bags that spread very rapidly in 2018 shows the power of the media in spreading the message. Besides using social media and in-store display, fashion brands can put across their message by making more use of that most basic of things – the hangtag on a garment – to pass on a sustainable message.

4. Inclusivity

Fenty Beauty, eloquently named after the last name of the singer, rose to fame very recently as a new thing. However, this is not a new idea. Brands like good old MAC, L'Oreal true match, Bobbi Brown, Lancôme and Iman Cosmetics have been around much longer. In fact, when Fenty Beauty's founder Rhianna was only 6 years old, in 1994, Iman founded her cosmetics line due to the scarcity of choice.

> Q: What can be learned from this is that the trend to communicate inclusivity to consumers and offer suitable products has been slowly growing over several decades, only to explode in the last years. Is it now at a level where consumers expect brands to have a stance on inclusivity and diversity? Can fashion truly be inclusive? Afterall, it is an industry that has a strong focus on the slim and beautiful, often fair-skinned and has a long-standing history of social exclusion.

> RT: Fashion has often played on social exclusion to incite consumer desire for product, but the Millennials are sophisticated and aware of the ways in which they are being played. Brands encouraging social inclusiveness – translating into a sense of 'brands for the people' – may become more important.

> There is absolutely no doubt in my mind that an emphasis on and provision for inclusivity and diversity are going to be long-term wins for fashion brands as well as society in general. Not all fashion brands can serve all consumers, but it is the spirit and intent that matter too. In this respect, the advertising campaigns under the United Colors banner for Italian knitwear brand Benetton by Oliviero Toscani in the 1980s were well ahead of their time. I met and interviewed Toscani during his golden years. He was an arch-provocateur, always with a twinkle in his eye. By the end of his time at Benetton, he appeared to have run out of steam.

> In the future, brands may even play a political role in a charged global political landscape: brand advertising has the power to be much more than simply a means of selling product. Expect to see the braver ones stand up for liberal values in an illiberal climate.

5. Emerging markets and global outlook for the next generations

The next important generations that fashion marketers will have to address are Gen Z and Gen Alpha who will presumably grow up with an understanding of sustainability and inclusivity, AI and new communications channels as well as gadgets, and a form of emotional and educated consumerism, making it vital for brands to tap into that demographic group with the right communications and marketing approach. Furthermore, these young consumers will be based from emerging economies which offer great opportunities but also challenges to brands.

Q: How do you perceive the future in this global and young world? And what must fashion brands consider in order to thrive in the future?

RT: The challenge will be how to bring together emotion, human 'realness' and the advantages of technology to connect with Gen Z and Gen Alpha. The young consumers in urban China and south-east Asia are extremely sophisticated in their use of technology, but there are also concerns over surveillance and the lack of privacy, which may create a more wary kind of consumer. The value and enjoyment of social interaction in the physical space of the shopping mall or flagship store will lead to a comeback of bricks-and-mortar stores driven by a new generation of retailers who blend the selling of product with entertainment and experiential fun.

An ethical future?

In several languages, the word for morning is very similar or nearly identical to the word for tomorrow. (In German "Morgen" means tomorrow but it also means morning.) Each morning is the start of our tomorrow and it is up to us to make it a good one. With every historical era, things changed, things improved or got worse. Occasionally this led to improvements or regulations that have ensured a better tomorrow for many people. Since we can predict only some elements of the future, we should at least predict our own behaviour and integrity.

Working in marketing and business, including the fashion industry, will inadvertently present us with questions for ethical consideration. Looking at future trends in particular, it is up to this and the next generation to decide how deeply we dive into the brain functions of humans, whether artificial intelligence would pose a security threat, how much marketers should manipulate emotions, exploit our insecurities, harm nature and populations for the sake of making a profit.

However, businesses have the option of introducing and adhering to fair and responsible practices. Porter and Kramer (2011) suggested a business model based on Creating Shared Value (CSV) that changes the concept of capitalism which is purely profit-driven and instead incorporates ethical values into its very core. The idea is that healthy businesses are directly linked to the surrounding communities with which a mutually respectful and fair partnership should be established. The authors question the profit driven values of companies: "How else could companies overlook the well-being of their customers, the depletion

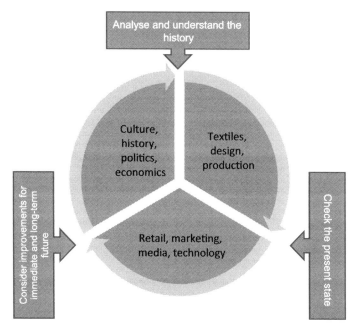

Figure 10.4 The Fashion Carousel revisited with Ethical Considerations. Author's original illustration.

of natural resources vital to their businesses, the viability of key suppliers, or the economic distress of the communities in which they produce and sell?" (Porter and Kramer, 2011, p.64).

The CSV concept has not been introduced into marketing and business practice as much as it could, mostly due to its setbacks in immediate profit, although some elements of the more commonly known Corporate Social Responsibility (CSR) are widely acknowledged. Fashion companies such as Patagonia, Brunello Cuccinelli, Loewe and Stella McCartney are positive trend-setters for incorporating ethical values into the core of its business. When working in the fashion industry, it is also a question of personal choice: To analyse and understand its history, its present state and consider improvements for the immediate and long-term ethical future.

Further reading

Bartlett, D. (2013) *Fashion Media: Past and Present*. London: Bloomsbury Academic.
Coleman, R. et al. (2007) *Design for Inclusivity: A Practical Guide to Accessible, Innovative and User-Centred Design (Design for Social Responsibility)*. Abingdon, UK: Routledge.

Holland, G. and Jones, R. (2017) *Fashion Trend Forecasting*. London: Laurence King Publishing.

Kondratiev, N. D. (2014) *The Long Waves in Economic Life. Reprint of 1935 English Translation.* Eastford, CT: Martino Fine Books.

Mason, H. (2015) *Trend-Driven Innovation: Beat Accelerating Customer Expectations.* John Wiley & Sons.

Murphy, P. E., Laczniak, G. R. and Harris, F. (2016) *Ethics in Marketing.* Abingdon, UK: Routledge.

O'Neill, M. (2017) *The Future is Now: 23 Trends That Will Prove Key to Business and Life.* London: Matt Publishing.

Porter, M. E. and Kramer M. R. (2011, January–February) The Big Idea: Creating Shared Value, Rethinking Capitalism. *Harvard Business Review* 89(1/2), 62–77.

Raymond, M. (2010) *The Trend Forecasters Handbook.* London: Laurence King Publishing.

WGSN www.wgsn.com/en

Stylus www.stylus.com

Nelli Rody www.nellyrodi.com/en

Trendstop www.trendstop.com

Bibliography and further reading

4A's (2019) *Home Page – 4A's*. Available at: www.aaaa.org/ [Accessed 22 May 2016].

Aaf.org (2019) *WHO WE ARE | AAF*. Available at: www.aaf.org/iMIS/AAFMemberR/WHO_ WE_ARE/AAFMemberR/Who_We_Are/Who%20We%20Are.aspx?hkey=40e639f5- 03ef-4f0d-aee5-806cc047ae68 [Accessed 2 Jul. 2016].

Abrahamian, A. (2019) Rise in Advertising as North Korea Embraces Nascent Consumerism. *The Guardian*. Available at: www.theguardian.com/world/2016/jun/17/rise-in-advertising- as-north-korea-embraces-nascent-consumerism [Accessed 20 Jun. 2016].

Advertising Research Foundation (2019) *The ARF*. Available at: https://thearf.org/ [Accessed 20 Dec. 2016].

Airbus.com (2004) *Flight Operation Briefing Notes*. Available at: www.airbus.com/fileadmin/ media_gallery/files/safety_library_items/AirbusSafetyLib_-FLT_OPS-HUM_PER- SEQ04.pdf [Accessed 6 Jul. 2015].

Akbareian, E. (2015) American Apparel's New CEO on Making the Brand Less Suggestive. *The Independent*. Available at: www.independent.co.uk/life-style/fashion/news/american- apparels-new-ceo-set-to-tone-down-the-brands-sexualised-imagery-10038459.html [Accessed 20 Jun. 2016].

Amos, C., Holmes, G. and Strutton, D. (2008) Exploring the Relationship between Celebrity Endorser Effects and Advertising Effectiveness: A Quantitative Synthesis of Effect Size. *International Journal of Advertising* 27(2), 209–234. DOI: 10.1080/02650487.2008.11073052

Amosa, A. and Haglund, M. (2002) From Social Taboo to "Torch of Freedom": The Marketing of Cigarettes to Women. *Tobacco Control* 9, 3–8. Available at: https://tobaccocontrol.bmj. com/content/tobaccocontrol/9/1/3.full.pdf [Accessed 12 Jun. 2016].

The ANDYs (2019) *About – ANDY Awards*. Available at: www.andyawards.com/about/ [Accessed 2 Jul. 2016].

Awasthi, A. K. and Choraria, S. (2015) Effectiveness of Celebrity Endorsement Advertisements: The Role of Customer Imitation Behaviour. *Journal of Creative Communications* 10(2), 215–234. Available at: https://doi.org/10.1177/0973258615597412

Bartlett, D., Cole, S. and Rocamora, A. (2013) *Fashion Media*. London: Bloomsbury.

Belfanti, C. (2008) Was Fashion a European Invention? *Journal of Global History* 3(3), 419–443.

Berlendi, C. (2011) *The Role of Social Media Within the Fashion and Luxury Industries*. Saarbrücken: Lap Lambert Academic.

Bischoff, W. (2006) *"Grenzenlose Räume"–Überlegungen zum Verhältnis von Architektur und städtischem Geruchsraum*, From Outer Space: Architekturtheorie außerhalb der Disziplin (Teil 2) 10. Jg., Heft 2, September 2006. Wolkenkuckucksheim – Cloud-Cuckoo-Land – Vozdushnyi Zamok Available at: www.cloud-cuckoo.net/openarchive/wolke/deu/Themen/052/Bischoff/bischoff.htm [Accessed 20 Sept. 2015].

Boumphrey, S. (2015) Strategies for Consumer Market Success in China. Euromonitor Market Research Blog. Available at: http://blog.euromonitor.com/2015/08/strategies-for-consumer-market-success-in-china.html [Accessed 15 Mar. 2017].

Breward, C. (1994) Femininity and Consumption: The Problem of the Late Nineteenth-Century Fashion Journal. *Journal of Design History* 7(2), 71–89. Available at: www.jstor.org/stable/1316078 [Accessed 2 Jul. 2016].

Bruhn, M. and Köhler, R. (2011) *Wie Marken wirken*. München: Franz Vahlen.

Caird, J. (2016) "A Character That Will Live Forever": How We Made the Levi's Flat Eric Ads. *The Guardian*. Available at: www.theguardian.com/media-network/2016/mar/31/levis-flat-eric-advert-puppet [Accessed 6 Jun. 2016].

Carter, C. and Steiner, L. (2004) *Critical Readings: Media and Gender*. Maidenhead: Open University Press (McGraw-Hill Education).

Cartner-Morley, J. (2012) Victoria's Secret v Agent Provocateur: Lingerie Stores Turn Up the Heat. *The Guardian*. Available at: www.theguardian.com/fashion/2012/oct/23/lingerie-agent-provocateur-victorias-secret

Castro, R. and Lewis, T. (2011) *Corporate Aviation Management*. Southern Illinois University Press.

Claritas (2015) MyBestSegments. Available at: https://segmentationsolutions.nielsen.com/mybestsegments/Default.jsp?ID=30&menuOption=segmentdetails&pageName=Segment%2BExplorer&id1=CLA.PNE [Accessed 7 Jan. 2017].

Collister, P. (2015) The Directory Big Won Rankings 2015. *The Directory*. Available at: www.directnewideas.com/bigwon/ [Accessed 9 Sept. 2016].

Cope, J. and Maloney, D. (2016) *Fashion Promotion in Practice*. New York: Fairchild.

Cortese, A. J. (1999) *Provocateur: Images of Women and Minorities in Advertising*. Boston: Rowman & Littlefield.

Cozens, C. (2003) Barnardo's Shock Ads Spark 330 Complaints. *The Guardian*. Available at: www.theguardian.com/media/2003/nov/24/advertising2 [Accessed 7 Jan. 2017].

Crestodina, A. (2018) Blogging Statistics and Trends: The 2018 Survey of 1000+ Bloggers. Available at: www.orbitmedia.com/blog/blogger-trends/

Cull, N. J., Culbert, D. and Welsh, D. (2003) *Propaganda and Mass Persuasion: A Historical Encyclopedia, 1500 to the Present*. ABC-Clio Inc.

Cullers, R. (2012) Ikea "Regrets" Airbrushing Women Out of Its Saudi Catalog. *Adweek*. Available at: www.adweek.com/adfreak/ikea-regrets-airbrushing-women-out-its-saudi-catalog-144140 [Accessed 10 Jun. 2015].

Curtis, A. (2011) *Five Years After Banning Outdoor Ads, Brazil's Largest City Is More Vibrant Than Ever*. Center for a New American Dream. Available at: www.newdream.org/resources/sao-paolo-ad-ban [Accessed 3 Jun. 2016].

Dejean, M. (2014) *Pourquoi supprimer les pubs des rues? Le maire de Grenoble répond* 25/11/14 15h44 Les Inrockuptibles. Available at: www.lesinrocks.com/2014/11/25/actualite/suppression-pub-rues-grenoble-on-retrouve-lidentite-reelle-ville-11537533/ [Accessed 3 Nov. 2016].

Desmet, D. et al. (2015) Speed and Scale: Unlocking Digital Value in Customer Journeys. Available at: www.mckinsey.com/insights/operations/speed_and_scale_unlocking_digital_value_in_customer_journeys?cid=digital-eml-alt-mip-mck-oth-1511

Diamond, J. (2015) *Retail Advertising and Promotion*. New York: Fairchild.

Drury, G. H. (1985) *The Historical Guide to North American Railroads*. Milwaukee: Kalmbach Publishing Co.

DynamicAction (2015) Now You're Talking: Four Customer Segmentation Secrets Revealed by Agent Provocateur. Available at: www.dynamicaction.com/now-youre-talking-four-customer-segmentation-secrets-revealed-by-agent-provocateur/

Ellis, N. et al. (2011) *Marketing:A Critical Textbook*. London: Sage Publications.

Epstein, E. J. (1982) Have You Ever Tried to Sell a Diamond? *The Atlantic*. Available at: www.theatlantic.com/magazine/archive/1982/02/have-you-ever-tried-to-sell-a-diamond/304575/

Fennis, B. M. and Stroebe, W. (2010) *The Psychology of Advertising*. Psychology Press.

Friedman, U. (2015) How an Ad Campaign Invented the Diamond Engagement Ring. *The Atlantic*, 13 Feb. Available at: www.theatlantic.com/international/archive/2015/02/how-an-ad-campaign-invented-the-diamond-engagement-ring/385376/ [Accessed 28 Aug. 2016].

Garber, M. (2015) "You've Come a Long Way, Baby": The Lag Between Advertising and Feminism. *The Atlantic*. Available at: www.theatlantic.com/entertainment/archive/2015/06/advertising-1970s-womens-movement/395897/

Goffman, E. (1976) *Gender Advertisements*. New York: Harper Torchbooks.

Grazia (2018) *Grazia*: An Eclectic Mix of Fashion, Beauty, Current Affairs and News that Celebrates Women. Available at: www.bauermedia.co.uk/uploads/Grazia.pdf [Accessed 1 Jan. 2019].

Higgins, D. (2015) Plan Ahead When Importing Goods to Your Doorstep. Available at: www.japanupdate.com/2015/01/plan-ahead-when-importing-goods-to-your-doorstep/

Hoang, L. (2016) Can Cost-Cutting Save Fashion Magazines? *Business of Fashion*. Available at: www.businessoffashion.com/articles/intelligence/cost-cutting-fashion-magazines-hearst-time-inc-conde-nast?utm_source=Subscribers&utm_campaign=ce6e732d6e-&utm_medium=email&utm_term=0_d2191372b3-ce6e732d6e-418254849

Holland, G. and Jones, R. (2017) *Fashion Trend Forecasting*. London: Laurence King Publishing.

Howley, C. L. (2009) Dressing a Virgin Queen: Court Women, Dress, and Fashioning the Image of England's Queen Elizabeth I. *Early Modern Women* 4, 201–208.

Jackson, T. and Shaw, D. (2009) *Mastering Fashion Marketing*. Basingstoke: Palgrave Macmillan.

Jhally, S. and Kilbourne, J. (1979) *Killing Us Softly: Advertising's Image of Women*. San Francisco: Kanopy Streaming, 2014.

Karolini, D. (2015) the6milliondollarstory. Available at: www.the6milliondollarstory.com/dont-crack-under-pressure-feat-cara-delevigne-for-tag-heuer/

Kawamura, Y. (2005) *Fashion-Ology: An Introduction to Fashion Studies*. New York: Berg.

Keaney, M. (2007) *Fashion and Advertising (World's Top Photographers Workshops)*.RotoVision.

Kendall, N. (2015) *What is a 21st Century Brand? New Thinking from the Next Generation of Agency Leaders*. London: Kogan Page.

Kenton, W. (2018, Feb.) Kondratieff Wave. Investopedia. Available at: www.investopedia.com/terms/k/kondratieff-wave.asp

KesselsKramer (2013) *Advertising for People Who Don't Like Advertising*. London: Laurence King Publishing.

Kilbourne, J. (1999) *Can't Buy ME Love: How Advertising Changes the Way We Think and Feel*. New York: Touchstone.

Kloss, I. (2012) *Werbung: Handbuch für Studium und Praxis*. 5th edn. München: Vahlen.

Kotler, P. (2012). Chicago Humanities Festival. Available at: http://chicagohumanities. org/events/2012/america/marketing-with-philip-kotler [from a conference recording] [Accessed 5 Jun. 2016].

Kotler, P. et al. (2009) *Marketing Management*. 13th edn. Harlow: Pearson Education Ltd.

Laird, P. (2001) *Advertising Progress: American Business and the Rise of Consumer Marketing*. Baltimore: Johns Hopkins University Press.

Lane, W. R., Whitehill, K. K. and Russel, T. J. (2008) *Kleppner's Advertising Procedure*. 17th edn. New Jersey: Pearson Prentice Hall.

Lea-Greenwood, G. (2012) *Gaynor: Fashion Marketing Communications*. John Wiley & Sons.

Lemelson, MIT. Massachusetts Institute of Technology. Available at: http://lemelson.mit. edu/resources/henry-ford [Accessed 18 Jun. 2016].

Levinson, J. C. (2016) Guerilla Marketing. Available at: www.gmarketing.com/index.php

Lewino, F. and Dos Santos, G. (2015) Les trois versions de "La Sortie des usines Lumière". *Le Point*. Available at: www.lepoint.fr/culture/les-trois-versions-de-la-sortie-des-usines-lumiere-27-03-2015-1916316_3.php [Accessed 23 Nov. 2016].

Life Magazine (1947) 14 Apr. 1947. Available at: https://books.google.de/books?id=ik0EAA AAMBAJ&pg=PA60&lpg=PA60&dq=adler%27s+elevator+shoes&source=bl&ots=Eti qRxsR9A&sig=w8pDcM2faZM-imh6ZtuvZR9iNfg&hl=en&sa=X&ved=0ahUKEwi9-f-jzdbNAhVK7xQKHdsxDHMQ6AEIcDAP#v=onepage&q=adler%27s%20elevator%20 shoes&f=false [Accessed 3 Jul. 2016].

London, B. (2015) As Celebrities Lead the Trend for Genderless Fashion, Selfridges Axes its Separate Women and Menswear Departments in Favour of Three Floors of Unisex Clothes. *Daily Mail*. Available at: www.dailymail.co.uk/femail/article-3002605/As-celebrities-lead-trend-genderless-fashion-Selfridges-axes-separate-women-menswear-departments-favour-three-floors-unisex-fashion.html [Accessed 28 Dec. 2016].

Macmillan Dictionary (2019) Propagate. Available at www.macmillandictionary.com/dictionary/british/propagate [Accessed 3 Jan. 2019].

Macmillan Dictionary (2019) Propaganda. Available at: www.macmillandictionary.com/dictionary/british/propaganda [Accessed 3 Jan. 2019].

Manral, K. (2011) The Difference between Above-the-Line and Below-the-Line Advertising. Available at: www.theadvertisingclub.net/index.php/features/editorial/3256-difference-between-above-the-line-and-below-the-line-advertising

Marketing-Schools (2012) Marketing with Celebrities: How to use Celebrities in Advertising. Available at: www.marketing-schools.org/consumer-psychology/marketing-with-celebrities.html [Accessed 7 Nov. 2015].

Mau, D. (2014) The 2014 September Issues by the Numbers. *Fashionista*. 23 Jul. Available at: http://fashionista.com/2014/07/september-issue-ad-pages

McGill (2019) *What is Sustainability?* Available at: www.mcgill.ca/sustainability/files/sustainability/what-is-sustainability.pdf

Merriam-Webster (2019) Ethic. Available at: www.merriam-webster.com/dictionary/ethic [Accessed 8 Feb. 2019].

Mintel (2015) 56% of Americans Stop Buying From Brands They Believe Are Unethical. Available at: www.mintel.com/press-centre/social-and-lifestyle/56-of-americans-stop-buying-from-brands-they-believe-are-unethical [Accessed 2 Aug. 2018].

Moore, G. (2012) *Basics Fashion Management: Fashion Promotion 02: Building a Brand through Marketing and Communication.* Lausanne: AVA Publishing.

Müller, S. and Gelbrich, K. (2015) *Interkulturelles Marketing.* Munich, Germany: Vahlen.

Muratodvski, G. (2011) The Role of Architecture and Integrated Design in City Branding. *Place Branding and Public Diplomacy* 8(3), 195–207.

Muratore, P. (2014) Ad People, Don't Get Stiffed by Dead Celebrities. *AdAge*. Available at: http://adage.com/article/cmo-strategy/marketers-beware-dead-celebs-ads/292427

Noel, C. P. (2010) Shock Advertising: Theories, Risks, and Outcomes Analyzed Using the Case of Barnardo's. *Inquiries Journal/Student Pulse.* Available at: www.inquiriesjournal.com/a?id=305

NRS (2015) National Readership Survey: Social Grade. Available at: www.nrs.co.uk/nrs-print/lifestyle-and-classification-data/social-grade/ [Accessed 20 Aug. 2015].

Nudd, T. (2016) Diesel Awkwardly Stuffs Every Online Obsession Into a New Global Ad Campaign. *AdWeek*,19 Jan. Available at: www.adweek.com/adfreak/diesel-awkwardly-stuffs-every-online-obsession-new-global-ad-campaign-169067

Oxford College of Marketing (2013) The Extended Marketing Mix: Physical Evidence. Available at: https://blog.oxfordcollegeofmarketing.com/2013/08/09/marketing-mix-physical-evidence-cim-content/ [Accessed 20 Nov. 2018].

Oyster (2011) Scott Schuman Makes Lots of Money and Hates Girls. *Oystermag*, 1 Oct. Available at: www.oystermag.com/scott-schuman-makes-lots-of-money-and-hates-girls#1RsX2TqmsjKk5qZL.99

Perlman, S. and Sherman, G. J. (2010) *Fashion Public Relations.* New York: Fairchild.

Posner, H. (2011). *Marketing Fashion.* New York: Laurence King Publishing.

Pouillard, V. (2013) The Rise of Fashion Forecasting and Fashion Public Relations, 1920–1940: The History of Tobe and Bernays, in Hartmut, B. and T. Kühne (eds.), *Globalizing Beauty: Consumerism and Body Aesthetics in the Twentieth Century.* Palgrave Macmillan, pp. 151–169.

Pravda (2007) Bomb Explodes at McDonald's Restaurant in St.Petersburg. *Pravda*, 19 Feb. Available at: www.pravdareport.com/news/hotspots/87528-mcdonalds

PRSA (2016) About Public Relations. Available at: www.prsa.org/aboutprsa/publicrelationsdefined/#.V3jWvKLdIq8 [Accessed 30 Aug. 2016].

Raimund, L. (2008) *Consumers: In a State of Sensory Overload.* Munich, Germany: Grin Verlag.

Rao, A. (2010) Second TVC for Cadbury Dairy Milk's "Shubh Aarambh" Released. *Campaign India*, 6 Sep. Available at: www.campaignindia.in/article/second-tvc-for-cadbury-dairy-milks-shubh-aarambh-released/412695

Remy, N., Catena, M. and Durand-Servoingt, B. (2015) Digital Inside: Get Wired for the Ultimate Luxury Experience. McKinsey&Company, Jul. Available at: www.mckinsey.com/~/media/mckinsey/industries/consumer%20packaged%20goods/our%20insights/is%20luxury%20ecommerce%20nearing%20its%20tipping%20point/digital_inside_full_pdf.ashx [Accessed 11 Sept. 2016].

Rigby, D. K. (2015) Customer Segmentation. Bain & Capital, 10 Jun. Available at: www.bain.com/Images/BAIN_GUIDE_Management_Tools_2015_executives_guide.pdf

Ryan, P. (2016) A Brand Case Study: The Superdry Appeal. *The Branding Journal*. Available at: www.thebrandingjournal.com/2016/03/the-superdry-appeal/

Scheier, C. and Held, D. (2006) *Wie Werbung wirkt: Erkenntnisse des Neuromarketing*. Munich, Germany: Haufe Lexware Gmbh.

Scheier, C. and Held, D. (2012) *Was Marken erfolgreich macht: Neuropsychologie in der Markenführung*. Munich, Germany: Haufe Lexware Gmbh.

Seto, F. (2017) How Does Trend Forecasting Really Work? *High Snobiety*, 5 Apr. Available at: www.highsnobiety.com/2017/04/05/trend-forecasting-how-to/

Sharma, A. (2016) How Predictive AI Will Change Shopping. *Harvard Business Review*, 18 Nov. Available at: https://hbr.org/2016/11/how-predictive-ai-will-change-shopping [Accessed 25 Nov. 2016].

SINUS Markt- und Sozialforschung GmbH (2015) Information on Sinus Milieus. Available at: www.sinus-institut.de/fileadmin/user_data/sinus-institut/Downloadcenter/20150805/2015-01-15_Information_on_Sinus-Milieus_English_version.pdf

Smith, P. R. and Zook, Z. (2016) *Marketing Communications: Offline and Online Integration, Engagement and Analytics*. 6th edn. London: Kogan Page.

Statista (2016) Anzeigenumsätze (brutto) der Elle in den Jahren 2010 bis 2018 (in Millionen Euro). Available at: http://de.statista.com/statistik/daten/studie/486439/umfrage/anzeigenumsaetze-der-frauenzeitschrift-elle/ [Accessed 11 Sept. 2016].

Statista (2018) Global Advertising Market – Statistics & Facts. Available at: www.statista.com/topics/990/global-advertising-market [Accessed 2 Feb. 2018].

Stutchbury, P. (2016) Architecture Foundation Australia and the Glenn Murcutt Master Class. Available at: www.ozetecture.org/2012/peter-stutchbury [Accessed 3 Dec. 2016].

Taflinger, R. F. (2011) Advantage: Consumer Psychology and Advertising. Kendall Hunt. Available at: https://online.vitalsource.com/#/books/9781465252685

Taylor, J. (2015) The Many Muses of Karl Lagerfeld, From Kendall Jenner to Tilda Swinton. *Observer*, 18 Aug. Available at: http://observer.com/2015/08/the-many-muses-of-karl-lagerfeld-from-kendall-jenner-to-tilda-swinton/ [Accessed 10 Feb. 2016].

Tungate, M. (2007) *Adland: A Global History of Advertising*. London: Kogan Page.

Tye, L. (2002) *The Father of Spin: Edward L. Bernays and the Birth of Public Relations*. New York: Henry Holt (Owl Books).

UN Broadband Commission (2016) China, India Now World's Largest Internet Markets. Unescopress, 15 Sep. Available at: www.unesco.org/new/en/media-services/single-view/news/china_india_now_worlds_largest_internet_markets [Accessed 9 Oct. 2016].

University of Twente (2017) *Two Step Flow Theory*. Available at: www.utwente.nl/en/bms/communication-theories/sorted-by-cluster/Mass-Media/Two_Step_Flow_Theory-1

Vecchi, A. and Buckley, C. (eds.) (2016) *Handbook of Research on Global Fashion Management and Merchandising*. Hershey, PN: IGI Global.

Villani, S. (2001) Impact of Media on Children and Adolescents: A 10-Year Review of the Research.*Journal of the American Academy of Child & Adolescent Psychiatry* 40(4), 392–401.

Wang, H. (2016) #Brand Transliteration: How to Translate and Protect Your Brand for the Chinese Market. CCPIT Patent and Trademark Law Office. Available at: www.ccpit-patent.com.cn/node/3795

Whitelock, A. (2013) *Elizabeth's Bedfellows*. London: Bloomsbury Publishing.

Williamson, J. (1978) *Decoding Advertisements: Ideology and Meaning in Advertising*. London: Marion Boyars.

Wind, Y. and Douglas, S. P. (2001) International Market Segmentation. Wharton School, University of Pennsylvania and CESA. Available at: https://faculty.wharton.upenn.edu/wp-content/uploads/2012/04/7213_International_Market_Segmentation.pdf

Winship, J. (1987) *Inside Womens' Magazines*. London: Pandora.

Yiddish Radio Project (2002) Sound Portraits Productions. Available at: www.yiddishradioproject.org [Accessed 12 Jun. 2016].

Yiddish Radio Project (2002) Exhibits. Sound Portraits Productions. Available at: www.yiddishradioproject.org/exhibits/history [Accessed 12 Jun. 2016].

Yurchisin, J. and Johnson, K. K. P. (2010) *Fashion and the Consumer*. Oxford: Berg.

Zarella, K. K. (2016) Diesels Renzo Rosso isn't Crazy just Genius. *Fashion Unfiltered*. Available at: http://fashionunfiltered.com/news/2016/diesel-s-renzo-rosso-isn-t-crazy-just-genius

Zeit Online (2012) Im Dienste der Werbung: Annoncen-Expeditionen feiern ihr hundertjähriges Bestehen. *DieZeit*, 17/1955. Available at: www.zeit.de/1955/17/im-dienste-der-werbung [Accessed 12 Jun. 2016].

Index